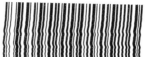

WISDOM,

INSIGHT

&

COUNSEL

WISDOM, INSIGHT & COUNSEL

365 DAILY
MEDITATIONS
COMPILED AND EDITED
BY DEBBY GULLERY

PARAGON HOUSE
NEW YORK

First Edition, 1995

Published in the United States by
Paragon House
370 Lexington Avenue,
New York, NY, 10017

Copyright © 1995 by Debby Gullery

A Thornwood Press Book

All rights reserved. No part of this publication may be reproduced in any form without the prior written permission of the publishers, unless by a reviewer who wishes to quote brief passages.

ISBN 1-55778-725-5 paperback

For Library of Congress Cataloging-in-Publication Data

Library of Congress
Cataloging-in-Publication Division,
Washington D.C. 20540-4320
(202) 707-5000

Cover & Book Design: Abel Graphics

Introduction

> Normal day, let me be aware of the treasure you are. Let me learn from you, love you, bless you before you depart. Let me not pass you by in quest of some rare and perfect tomorrow. Let me hold you while I may, for it may not always be so. One day I shall dig my nails into the earth, or bury my face in the pillow, or stretch myself taut, or raise my hands to the sky and want, more than all the world, your return.
> — Mary Jean Irion, *Yes, World*

All of us are busy, and we wear many hats. I am a wife and mother of three children. I have a job that I love as chairwoman of a non-profit organization. Involvement in my community, the children's schools, their playdates and activities, and my congregation, all add to the demands on whatever time I have.

I've realized that the true art of life lies in finding the balance between ordinary daily activities and the ideals which inspire me to do more and to do better.

Recently a friend shared this story with me: Her husband works in an office which overlooks the Hudson River. One evening he was so moved by the beauty of the sunset that he called her at home, emphatic that she run out and see it. This mother of two toddlers was in the middle of post-dinner clean-up. She did go outside, and was impressed, but later told me that she couldn't really stop long enough to connect to the beauty and allow it to nourish and fill her. I truly felt her heart, having had similar experiences.

I've also been blessed with happier occasions. Recently I had scheduled a walk to the brook with my four-year old. It was a perfect autumn day. Toby and I played hide-and-seek, and later I sat by the brook and watched him chase the falling leaves. I was filled with the desire to just stop and *be* in the moment, to drink the perfect joy of it deep into my soul and I did!

Experiences like these help me to remember the value of nurturing the ability to be still and be filled, of finding a quiet moment every day. That, then, is the purpose of this book — to offer an inspiration or thought that can provide a focus, if only for a few moments, on what is truly important.

I've always been moved by the written word, drawing lines around inspiring quotes, putting

Wisdom, Insight & Counsel

pieces of paper in library books so that I could copy the passages out later, which I seldom did.

This book, however, has enabled me to do just that — go back to all those books, poems and songs which touched my heart or stirred my soul, gleaning the best and offering them.

I know that they will give you some of what they gave me: an inner sanctuary and a vision of what's possible each day.

Special thanks to my husband and three children who supported and encouraged me through months of research. To both my parents who gave me a "heart start" in life. And to my God, who created the potential for all the inspiration, beauty and love in the world.

Debby Gullery

January 1

I have a few ideas that I think are very useful to me. One is that you do whatever comes your way as well as you can, and another is that you think as little as possible about yourself and as much as possible about other people and about things that are interesting. The third is that you get more joy out of giving joy to others and should put a good deal of thought into the happiness that you are able to give.
— Eleanor Roosevelt

JANUARY 2

IF I CAN STOP ONE HEART FROM BREAKING
Emily Dickinson

If I can stop one heart from breaking,
I shall not live in vain;
If I can ease one life the aching,
Or cool one pain,
Or help one fainting robin
Unto his nest again,
I shall not live in vain.

. . . . that best portion of a good man's life, his little, nameless, unremembered acts of kindness and of love.
— William Wordsworth

January 3

Nothing will ever be attempted, if all possible objections must be first overcome.
— Dr. Samuel Johnson, *Rasselas*

Now it is time for action. We must not wait until we can get the complete diagnosis. The complete diagnosis is an autopsy.
— Frederico Mayor

A man of words but not of deeds is like a garden full of weeds.

January 4

God is both within us and without us. He is the source of all life; the creator of universe behind universe; and of unimaginable depths of interstellar space and of light-years without end. But He is also the indwelling life of our own little selves. And just as a whole world full of electricity will not light a house unless the house itself is prepared to receive that electricity, so the infinite and eternal life of God cannot help us unless we are prepared to receive that life within ourselves. Only the amount of God that we can get in us will work for us.
— Agnes Sanford, *The Healing Light*

It is one thing to show a man that he is in error, and another to put him in possession of the truth.
— John Locke

We have a saying in Burmese, "If you try hard enough, you can become a Buddha." I was saying to the young people that you must all try, you must all try very hard to be as noble and elevated as possible.
— Daw Aung San Suu Kyi

January 6

Attitude is never a substitute for action, and thinking about something is never a substitute for doing it.
— Carolyn Warner

"Oh, I'm so glad," exulted Pollyanna. The game was to just find something about everything to be glad about — no matter what 'twas. . . . You see, when you're hunting for the glad things, you sort of forget the other kind.
— Eleanor H. Porter, *Pollyanna*

January 7

Problems are messages.
— Shakti Gawain

Yet it is in this whole process of meeting and solving problems that life has its meaning. Problems are the cutting edge that distinguishes between success and failure. Problems call forth our courage and our wisdom; indeed, they create our courage and our wisdom. It is only because of problems that we grow mentally and spiritually. When we desire to encourage the growth of the human spirit, we challenge and encourage the human capacity to solve problems, just as in school we deliberately set problems for our children to solve. It is through the pain of confronting and resolving problems that we learn. As Benjamin Franklin said, "Those things that hurt, instruct." It is for this reason that wise people learn not to dread but actually to welcome problems and actually to welcome the pain of problems.
— M. Scott Peck, M.D., *The Road Less Traveled*

January 8

Mystical awakening enables a person to experience an extension of consciousness, a release of power, a broadening of vision, so that aspects of truth beyond those of the rational intellect are available to him.
— Carol Ann Brooks

I sought for God for thirty years. I thought it was I who desired Him, but no, it was He who desired me.
— Abu Yazid

Learn to listen. Opportunity sometimes knocks very softly.
— H. Jackson Brown, Jr.

THE LION AND THE MOUSE
Aesop

One day a great lion lay asleep in the sunshine. A little mouse ran across his paw and wakened him. The great lion was just going to eat him up when the little mouse cried, "Oh, please, let me go, sir. Some day I may help you."

The lion laughed at the thought that the little mouse could be of any use to him. But he was a good-natured lion, and he set the mouse free.

Not long after, the lion was caught in a net. He tugged and pulled with all his might, but the ropes were too strong. Then he roared loudly. The little mouse heard him, and ran to the spot. "Be still, dear Lion, and I will set you free. I will gnaw the ropes."

With his sharp little teeth, the mouse cut the ropes, and the lion came out of the net.

"You laughed at me once," said the mouse. "You thought I was too little to do you a good turn. But see, you owe your life to a poor little mouse."

January 10

A clay pot sitting in the sun will always be a clay pot. It has to go through the white heat of the furnace to become porcelain.
— Mildred Witte Stouven

We cannot find peace if we are afraid of the windstorms of life.
— Elizabeth Kübler-Ross

January 11

The Human Touch
Spencer Michael Free

'Tis the human touch in this world that counts,
The touch of your hand and mine,
Which means far more to the fainting heart,
Than shelter and bread and wine;
For shelter is gone when the night is o'er,
And bread lasts only a day,
But the touch of the hand and the sound of the voice
Sing on in the soul alway.

January 12

What we want... is character.... It is a thing we must get for ourselves. We must labor for it. It is gained by toil—hard toil.... It is attainable; but we must attain it, and attain it each for himself. I cannot for you, and you cannot for me.
— Frederick Douglass

Character building begins in our infancy and continues until death.
— Eleanor Roosevelt

January 13

I want you to realize that the true relationship between God and man is a subject and object relationship. You are His sons and His daughters. Once you have achieved unity with God, nothing can trouble you. Neither sorrow nor loneliness, sickness or anything else under the sun can discourage you. God is the ultimate security. You could pay many millions of dollars and still not buy that kind of security. It is priceless. No money can buy it. This is the total experience of life. We are meant to live with God.

The quality of our lives is determined by the strength of our awareness of being God's child.
— Young Whi Kim

January 14

RESULTS AND ROSES
Edgar Guest

The man who wants a garden fair,
Or small or very big,
With flowers growing here and there,
Must bend his back and dig.

The things are mighty few on earth
That wishes can attain.
Whate'er we want of any worth
We've got to work to gain.

It matters not what goal you seek
Its secret here reposes:
You've got to dig from week to week
To get Results or Roses.

January 15

We must find our duties in what comes to us, not in what we imagine might have been.
— George Eliot

I long to accomplish a great and noble task, but it is my chief duty to accomplish small tasks as if they were great and noble.
— Helen Keller

January 16

Toward the end of his tragic, devoted life, General Robert E. Lee attended the christening of a friend's child. The mother asked him for a word that would guide the child along the road to manhood.

Lee's answer summed up the creed that had borne him, through struggle and suffering, to a great place in the American legend. "Teach him," he said simply, "to deny himself."

It is one thing to praise discipline, and another to submit to it.
— Miguel Cervantes

Just concentrate on helping one person, giving hope to one person, and that person in turn may give hope to somebody else and it will spread out.
— Aaron Abrahamsen

Life is not easy for any of us. But what of that? We must have perseverance and above all confidence in ourselves. We must believe that we are gifted for something, and that this thing, at whatever cost, must be attained.
— Marie Curie

January 18

Creating the unity necessary to run an effective business or a family or a marriage requires great personal strength and courage. No amount of technical administrative skill in laboring for the masses can make up for lack of nobility of personal character in developing relationships. It is at a very essential, one-on-one level that we live the primary laws of love and life.
— Stephen R. Covey

A great rock is not disturbed by the wind; the mind of a wise man is not disturbed by either honor or abuse.
— Buddha

January 19

Posterity — you will never know how much it has cost my generation to preserve your freedom. I hope you will make good use of it.
— John Quincy Adams

What we obtain too cheaply, we esteem too lightly; it is dearness only that gives everything its value. Heaven knows how to put a price upon its goods; and it would be strange indeed if so celestial an article as freedom should not be highly rated.
— Thomas Payne

January 20

The disciple Kung-too said, "All are equally men, but some are great men, and some are little men—how is this?" Mencius replied, "Those who follow that part of themselves which is great are great men; those who follow that part which is little are little men. To the mind belongs the office of thinking. By thinking, it gets the right view of things; by neglecting to think, it fails to do this. Let a man first stand fast in the supremacy of the nobler part of his constitution, and the inferior part will not be able to take it from him. It is simply this which makes the great man."
— Mencius

January 21

All who have meditated on the art of governing mankind are convinced that the fate of empires depends on the education of youth.
— Aristotle

The cure of crime is not the electric chair, but the high chair.
— J. Edgar Hoover

January 22

For us there was never a time when we did not believe in God. There's a lot in this world you can't see that you still believe in life, love and courage. Well, that's the way it is with faith. Just because you can't hold it in your hand doesn't mean its not there. A person who has faith is prepared for life and to do something with it.
— Sadie and Elizabeth Delaney,
The Book of Everyday Wisdom

So wherever I am, there's always Pooh,
There's always Pooh and Me.
"What would I do?" I said to Pooh,
"If it wasn't for you," and Pooh said: "True,
It isn't much fun for One, but Two
Can stick together," says Pooh, says he.
"That's how it is," says Pooh.
— A. A. Milne

We're here so that we can help each other to grow. When you step on a needle you put your two thumbs together and you try to push that needle back out. That is why we need each other — to push, to grow.
— Le Ly Hayslip

JANUARY 24

I sought my soul — but my soul I could not see;
I sought my God — but my God eluded me;
I sought my brother — and found all three.

God is love; he that dwells in love dwells in God, and God in him.
— St. John

If we really believed that those who are gone from us were as truly alive as ourselves, we could not invest the subject with such aweful depth of gloom as we do. If we could imbue our children with distinct faith in immortality, we should never speak of people as dead, but as passed into another world. We should speak of the body as a cast-off garment, which the wearer had outgrown; consecrated indeed by the beloved being that used it for a season, but of no value within itself.
— Lydia Maria Child, *Letters from New York*

January 26

One should basically know what is right and what is wrong — and, when you know that, be courageous enough to stand up for what is right.
— Nien Cheng

The greatest want of the world is the want of men — men who will not be bought or sold; men who in their inmost souls are true and honest; men who do not fear to call sin by its right name; men whose conscience is as true to duty as the needle to the pole; men who will stand for the right though the heavens fall.
— E. G. White

January 27

It makes no difference what background a person has, whether Indian or non-Indian. To all who have never felt accepted, who are living a life of loneliness, who seem to be unimportant to anyone — I am thrilled to say: God is love! His love is real and He loves and yearns to touch your life. That touch is important and God makes his contact through people, passing his love right now through me to you.
— Princess Pale Moon

January 28

I'll let you into the secret. It is nothing really difficult if you only begin. Some people contemplate a task until it looks so big it seems impossible, but I just begin and it gets done somehow. There would be no coral islands if the first bug sat down and began to wonder how the job was to be done.
— Josh Billings

The secret of getting ahead is getting started.
— Sally Berger

January 29

Integrate what you believe into every single area of your life. Take your heart to work and ask the most and best of everybody else. Don't let your special character and values, the secret that you know and no one else does, the truth — don't let that get swallowed up by the great chewing complacency.
— Meryl Streep

January 30

Difficulties are things that show what men are.
— Epictetus

To bear up under loss; to fight the bitterness of defeat and the weakness of grief; to be the victor over anger, to smile when tears are close; to resist disease and evil men and base instincts; to hate hate, and to love love, to go on when it would seem good to die; to look up with unquenchable faith in something ever more about to be — that is what any man can do, and be great.
— Zane Grey

January 31

Everyone in our culture desires to some extent to be loving, yet many are not in fact loving. I therefore conclude that the desire to love is not itself love. Love is as love does. Love is an act of will — namely, both an intention and an action. Will also implies choice. We do not have to love. We choose to love. No matter how much we may think we are loving, if we are in fact not loving, it is because we have chosen not to love and therefore do not love, despite our good intentions. On the other hand, whenever we do actually exert ourselves in the cause of spiritual growth, it is because we have chosen to do so. The choice to love has been made.
— M. Scott Peck, M.D., *The Road Less Traveled*

We can only learn to love by loving.
— Doris Murdock

February 1

"Why do you worry, Mr. Gruffydd?" I asked him, and hot with sorrow as soon as it was out. His eyes carried loads of darkness, and he saw with tiredness, and with patience that was willed, but not felt.

"Worry, my son?" he said, with quiet. "I am not worried now and I never have or will. You must learn to tell worry from thought, and thought from prayer. Sometimes a light will go from your life, Huw, and your life becomes a prayer, till you are strong enough to stand under the weight of your own thought again."

— Richard Llewellyn, *How Green Was My Valley*

February 2

He who prays for his fellow man, while he himself has the same need, will be answered first.
— Talmud, Baba Kamma

And when you pray you must not be like the hypocrites, for they love to stand and pray in the synagogues and at the street corners, that they may be seen by men. Truly, I say to you, they have received their reward. But when you pray, go into your room and shut the door and pray to your Father who is in secret; and your Father who sees in secret will reward you.
And in praying do not heap up empty phrases as the Gentiles do; for they think that they will be heard for their many words. Do not be like them, for your Father knows what you need before you ask them.
— Matthew, 6:5–8

February 3

Do men imagine that they will be left [at ease] because they say, "We believe," and will not be tested with affliction? Lo! We tested those who were before you. This God knows those who are sincere, and those who feign.
— Qur'an 29. 2–3

Purity of soul and nobility of character are the qualities that count in God's estimation of each man. Every man stands with his fellow men on a common footing before God.

If you wish to find the true way,
Right action will lead you to it directly;
But if you do not strive for Buddhahood
You will grope in the dark and never find it.
— Sutra of Hui Neng, 2

T'ai / Peace
Heaven exists on earth for those who
maintain correct thoughts and actions.
— I Ching

FEBRUARY 5

We know as winter approaches the wind blows very strongly and leaves drop off the trees. At times the limbs blow down or break. When again in the spring the wind blows, those trees, silent and completely bare in winter with no leaves, start to be gently rocked again. What kind of meaning does this have? In summer, the trees put forth their leaves in the top part of the tree, the part that grows most. Yet in the wintertime, the part that is growing is not seen. The roots grow during the wintertime, so when the trees shake in the wind as winter approaches, the sap which flowed freely all summer long begins to descend into the roots.

In our lives of faith there are times when we are blown by very strong winds and others when warm winds waft through us; different parts of us grow at different times. Therefore, we know that no matter how much of a struggle, how much of a wind is beating against us, if we just somehow endure and grow through that time of suffering, our hearts become much deeper. Then somehow we can survive.

All through our lives, we go through times of deep struggles and deep sacrifice, in order that our roots may grow.
— Shin Wook Kim

February 6

Perhaps the clearest mark of God's love is compassion. Compassion synthesizes fervent personal commitment with openness to others' points of view. It involves the action of caring for others while being rooted in the solitude of self-valuing and contemplation of the divine.

Compassion calls us to service. It asks us to actually help our fellow human beings. With compassion we walk the walk that we talk.

— John Bradshaw, *Creating Love*

February 7

It's wonderful to climb the liquid mountains of the sky. Behind me and before me is God and I have no fears.
— Helen Keller

I have three treasures. Guard them and keep them safe! The first is love; the second is moderation; the third is humility. From love one gains courage; from moderation one gains ability; from humility one achieves greatness. To forsake love and courage, to forsake moderation and ability, to forsake humility and rush to the forefront, is death to all hope.
With love battles can be won; with love defenses prove invulnerable; with love heaven arms those it would protect.
— Tao

February 8

Among all my patients in the second half of life — that is to say, over thirty-five — there has not been one whose problem in the last resort was not that of finding a religious outlook on life. It is safe to say that every one of them fell ill because he had lost that which the living religions of every age have given to their followers, and none of them has been really healed who did not regain his religious outlook.
— Carl G. Jung

February 9

Of all the traps and pitfalls in life, self-disesteem is the deadliest, and the hardest thing to overcome; for it is a pit designed and dug by our own hands, summed up in the phrase, "It's no use — I can't do it." . . . It is that good hard second look — taken not just for one's own sake but for everyone else's too — that very often reveals that the "impossible" task is quite possible after all.
— Maxwell Maltz

All growth, including political growth, is the result of risk-taking.
— Jude Wanniski

February 10

But as the rest of the world grew stranger, one thing became increasingly clear. And that was the reason the two of us were here. Why others should suffer we were not shown. As for us, from morning to lights-out, whenever we were not in ranks for roll call, our Bible was the center of an ever-widening circle of help and hope. Like waifs clustered around a blazing fire, we gathered about it, holding out our hearts to its warmth and light. The blacker the night around us grew, the brighter and truer and more beautiful burned the word of God.

Life in Ravensbruck took place on two separate levels, mutually impossible. One, the observable, external life, grew every day more horrible. The other, the life we lived with God, grew daily better, truth upon truth, glory upon glory.

— Corrie Ten Boom, *The Hiding Place*

FEBRUARY 11

It is necessary to try to surpass oneself always; this occupation ought to last as long as life.
— Christina, Queen of Sweden, 1629-89

It's not enough to be good if you have the ability to be better. It is not enough to be very good if you have the ability to be great.
— Alberta Lee Cox, Grade 8

February 12

Nothing that is worth doing is achieved in a lifetime; therefore, we must be saved by hope. Nothing which is true or beautiful or good makes complete sense in any immediate context of history; therefore, we must be saved by faith. Nothing we do, however virtuous, can be accomplished alone; therefore, we are saved by love.
— Reinhold Niebuhr

FEBRUARY 13

I wonder if heaven will not be a long gazing on a face ye canna tire of, but must ever have one more glimpse.
— Mary Webb

> You'll fly back like a sparrow,
> back to me
> Sailing 'cross the morning on the breeze
> But I never really miss you
> when you leave
> No, I only think about you
> when I breathe.
> — Sheila Vaughn

Spread love everywhere you go; first of all in your own home. Give love to your children, to your wife or husband, to your next door neighbor . . . . Let no one ever come to you without leaving better. Be the living expression of God's kindness; kindness in your face, kindness in your eyes, kindness in your smile, kindness in your warm greeting.
— Mother Teresa

February 15

Peace I ask of thee, O river,
peace, peace, peace.
When I learn to live serenely,
Cares will cease.
From the hills I gather courage
Vision of the day to be;
Strength to lead and faith to follow,
All are given unto me.
Peace I ask of thee, O river,
Peace, peace, peace.

February 16

Ultimately, we have just one moral duty: to reclaim large areas of peace in ourselves, more and more peace, and to reflect it toward others. And the more peace there is in us, the more peace there will be in our troubled world.
— Etty Hillesum

February 17

"Human beings do not live forever, Reuven. We live less than the time it takes to blink an eye, if we measure our lives against eternity. So it may be asked what value is there to a human life. There is so much pain in the world. What does it mean to have to suffer so much if our lives are nothing more than the blink of an eye?" He paused again, his eyes misty now, then went on. "I learned a long time ago, Reuven, that a blink of an eye in itself is nothing. But the eye that blinks, that is something. A span of life is nothing. But the man who lives that span, he is something. He can fill that tiny span with meaning, so its quality is immeasurable though its quantity may be insignificant. Do you understand what I am saying? A man must fill his life with meaning, meaning is not automatically given to life. It is hard work to fill one's life with meaning. That I do not think you understand yet. A life filled with meaning is worthy of rest. I want to be worthy of rest when I am no longer here. Do you understand what I am saying?"
— Chaim Potok, *The Chosen*

The purpose of life is a life of purpose.
— Robert Byrne

February 18

Are you a politician asking what your country can do for you, or a zealous one asking what you can do for your country? If you are the first, then you are a parasite; if the second, then you are an oasis in the desert.
— Kahlil Gibran, written in Arabic after WWII

Now the trumpet summons us again — not as a call to bear arms, though arms we need — not as a call to battle, though embattled we are — but a call to bear the burden of a long twilight struggle, year in and year out, "rejoicing in hope, patient in tribulation" — a struggle against the common enemies of man: tyranny, poverty, disease and war itself.
— John F. Kennedy

FEBRUARY 19

THE THINGS THAT HAVEN'T BEEN DONE BEFORE
Edgar Guest

A few strike out, without map or chart,
Where never a man has been,
From the beaten paths they draw apart
To see what no man has seen.
There are deeds they hunger alone to do;
Though battered and bruised and sore,
They blaze the path for the many, who
Do nothing not done before.

The things that haven't been done before
Are the tasks worthwhile today;
Are you one of the flock that follows, or
Are you one that shall lead the way?
Are you one of the timid souls that quail
At the jeers of a doubting crew,
Or dare you, whether you win or fail,
Strike out for a goal that's new?

As long as we think dugout canoes are the only possibility — all that is real or can be real-we will never see the ship, we will never feel the wind blow.
— Sonia Johnson

February 20

Time is the one commodity above all that is our true possession.... Time's most important quality is that it passes, that we have only a finite amount. Therefore, be aware of its value and know that when you give your time, you're giving of your life.
— Daphne Rose Kingma

February 21

Ideals are like stars: you will not succeed in touching them with your hands, but like the seafaring man on the desert of waters, you choose them as your guides, and following them you reach your destiny.
— Carl Schurz

February 22

I wonder how far Moses would have gone if he'd taken a poll in Egypt. What would Jesus Christ have preached if he'd taken a poll in Israel?... It isn't polls or public opinion of the moment that counts. It's right and wrong.
— Jef Raskin, *Wired*, September 1994

Still, if you will not fight for the right when you can easily win without bloodshed; if you will not fight when your victory will be sure and not too costly; you may come to the moment when you will have to fight with all the odds against you and only a precarious chance of survival. There may even be a worse case. You may have to fight when there is no hope of victory, because it is better to perish than live as slaves.
— Winston Churchill

February 23

Your life feels different on you, once you greet death and understand your heart's position. You wear your life like a garment from the mission bundle sale ever after — lightly because you realize you never paid nothing for it, cherishing because you know you won't ever come by such a bargain again.
— Louise Erdrich, *Love Medicine*

February 24

Man will only become better when you make him see what he is like.
— Chekhov, *Notebooks*

Repentance, to be of any avail, must work a change of heart and conduct.
— Theodore Ledyard Cuyler

FEBRUARY 25

The conventional explanation, that God sends us the burden because He knows that we are strong enough to handle it, has it all wrong. Fate, not God, sends us the problem. When we try to deal with it, we find out that we are not strong. We are weak; we get tired, we get angry, overwhelmed. We begin to wonder how we will ever make it through all the years. But when we reach the limits of our own strength and courage, something unexpected happens. We find reinforcement coming from a source outside of ourselves. And in the knowledge that we are not alone, that God is on our side, we manage to go on.
— Harold S. Kushner,
When Bad Things Happen to Good People

February 26

When one's own problems are unsolvable and all best efforts are frustrated, it is lifesaving to listen to other people's problems.
— Suzanne Massie

Like everyone else I feel the need of relations and friendship, of affection, of friendly intercourse, and I am not made of stone or iron, so I cannot miss these things without feeling, as does any other intelligent man, a void and deep need. I tell you this to let you know how much good your visit has done to me.
— Vincent Van Gogh, *Dear Theo*

February 27

Union is Strength

A certain man had several sons who were always quarreling with one another, and, try as he might, he could not get them to live together in harmony. So he determined to convince them of their folly by the following means. Bidding them fetch a bundle of sticks, he invited each in turn to break it across his knee. All tried and all failed: and then he undid the bundle, and handed them the sticks one by one, when they had no difficulty at all in breaking them.

"There, my boys," said he, "united you will be more than a match for your enemies: but if you quarrel and separate, your weakness will put you at the mercy of those who attack you."

— Aesop

February 28

He that studies only men, will get the body of knowledge without the soul; and he that studies only books, the soul without the body. He that to what he sees, adds observation, and to what he reads, reflection, is on the right road to knowledge, provided that in scrutinizing the hearts of others, he neglects not his own.
— Caleb Colton

March 1

Tomorrow is the most important thing in life. Comes into us at midnight. It's perfect when it arrives and it puts itself in our hands. It hopes we've learned something from yesterday.
— John Wayne

Daily Treasure
You wake up in the morning, and lo! your purse is magically filled with twenty-four hours of the unmanufactured tissue of the universe of your life. It is yours. It is the most precious of possessions. No one can take it from you. It is unstealable. And no one receives either more or less than you receive.
— Arnold Bennett

March 2

The House You Are Building

Every spirit builds itself a house, and beyond its house a world, and beyond its world a heaven. Know then that the world exists for you. For you is the phenomenon perfect.
What we are, that only can we see.
All that Adam had, all that Caesar could, you have and you can do. Adam called his house, heaven and earth. Caesar called his house, Rome.
You perhaps call yours a cobbler's trade; a scholar's garret. Yet line for line and point for point, your dominion is as great as theirs, though without fine names.
Build therefore your own world as fast as you can. Conform your life to the pure idea in your mind, that will unfold into great proportions.
— Ralph Waldo Emerson

March 3

Beloved is man, for he was created in the image of God. But it was by a special love that it was made known to him that he was created in the image of God.
— Mishnah, Abot 3.18

Do you know that you are God's temple and that God's Spirit dwells in you? . . . For God's temple is holy, and that temple you are.
— Galatians 2.20

March 4

It was then that I had thoughts about Christ, and I have never changed my mind. He did appear to me then as a man, and as a man I still think of him. In that way, I have had comfort. If he had been a God, or any more a son of God than any of us, then it is unfair to ask us to do what he did. But if he was a man who found out for himself what there is that is hidden in life, then we all have a chance to do the same. And with the help of God, we shall.

— Richard Llewellyn, *How Green Was My Valley*

March 5

A man is not idle because he is absorbed in thought. There is a visible labor and there is an invisible labor.
— Victor Hugo

I think and think for months and years. Ninety-nine times, the conclusion is false. The hundredth time I am right.
— Albert Einstein

MARCH 6

It never occurred to my Mama to define love. She would have laughed at the idea. Everything she did was a kind of loving act. She gave love in our home a tangible feeling. Her love for her children and husband was plainly evident. She was forever looking at us fondly, hugging us (over our false protestations), or sharing in our laughter or tears. She never saw my Papa as a saint, but she treated him as a very likely candidate. You could feel her high level of spiritual love; her every act, thought and deed was an affirmation of the presence of God.

Love, for Mama, was not something she thought or talked about. It was something she lived in action. She showed us, as Mother Teresa has, that love is found in sweeping a floor, cleaning a sink, caring for someone ill, or offering a comforting embrace.

— Leo Buscaglia, *Born for Love*

March 7

We live in a world where our power gives us the chance of doing unlimited harm; and we need an education which teaches us not merely how to use that power but how to use it well. To build up in every man and woman a solid core of spiritual life, which will resist the attrition of everyday existence in our mechanized world — that is the most difficult and important task of school and university. Barbarian tribes destroyed the Roman Empire. There are no such tribes to destroy modern civilization from outside. The barbarians are ourselves. The real problem is to humanize man, to show him the spiritual ideals without which neither happiness nor success is genuine or permanent, to produce beings who will know not merely how to split atoms but how to use their powers for good. Such knowledge is not to be had from the social or physical sciences.
— Sir Richard Livingstone,
Some Tasks for Education

To educate a man in mind and not in morals is to educate a menace to society.
— Theodore Roosevelt

March 8

You may not see yourself growing up, but you definitely know it when you are sinning.
— Akan Proverb (Ghana)

You can give without loving, but you cannot love without giving.
— Amy Carmichael

March 9

Man needs peace in his heart and mind. This is only possible when he is united with God; there is no other way. Our external circumstances may be hard, but if our heart is right with God, we will find peace. God wants to speak to us and guide us. How can we receive His guidance? If we have a pure heart, we can receive it from Him directly; otherwise God must teach us through someone else. It's best to know through our own heart, but if that's not possible, God will guide us through a third person. When we are open to accept any direction from God, He will work with us. If we are closed, however, He cannot reach us. So we must always keep the way open for God to enter and advise us. While God sees everything, our viewpoint is very narrow. So we want to see through His eyes.

MARCH 10

It is not the suffering that will end. As far as I can tell, the one thing we can count in is that everything we are counting on is going to fall through under us. I will never welcome the feeling of falling through the floor. But I believe we are falling through into God or something — but not nothing. I believe it is the whole from which we came and to which, deep down, we long to belong. I believe our longing is exceeded only by its longing for us.
— Polly Berrien Berens

Here on earth, children naturally long for their parents even when they are separated for only a few days. This human tendency comes from the original nature of man; we are longing for that one parent of mankind, God. This inseparable relationship must be reestablished because man cannot bear the loneliness of being separated from God.

March 11

An old man lived with his son in a fort. One day the son lost his horse. The neighbors rushed into the house to express their sympathy, but the old man said: "How do you know that this is bad luck?"

A few days later, the horse came back with a number of wild horses. So the neighbors flocked indoors to congratulate him, but the old man said: "How do you know this is good luck?"

Now that he had so many horses to ride, the son one day rode away on one of the wild horses. He fell off, breaking his leg. Again the neighbors knocked at the door to say: "Alas! Alas!" but the old man said: "Tut! Tut! How do you know this is bad luck?"

Sure enough, before many weeks had passed, there was a great war in the Middle Flowery Kingdom, but because the old man's son was crippled, he did not have to go off to fight.

— Chinese folk tale

This is my song, O God of all the nations,
A song of peace for lands afar and mine.
This is my home, the country where my heart is;
Here are my hopes, my dreams, my holy shrine;
But other hearts in other lands are beating
With hopes and dreams as true and high as mine.

My country's skies are bluer than the ocean,
And sunlight beams on cloverleaf and pine.
But other lands have sunlight too, and clover,
And skies are everywhere as blue as mine.
Oh, hear my song, thou God of all the nations,
A song of peace for their land and for mine.

March 13

To be wronged is nothing unless you continue to remember it.
— Confucius

I make it a practice to avoid hating anyone. If someone's been guilty of despicable actions, especially toward me, I try to forgive him. I used to follow a practice — somewhat contrived, I admit — to write the man's name on a piece of scrap paper, drop it into the lowest drawer of my desk, and say to myself: "That finishes the incident and, so far as I'm concerned, that fellow." The drawer became over the years a sort of private wastebasket for crumbled-up spite and discarded personalities.
— Dwight D. Eisenhower

March 14

As I go commonly sweeping the stair,
Doing my part of the everyday care,
Human and simple my lot and my share,
I am aware of a marvelous thing:
Voices that call me — voices that ring
From far lands of ocean on heavenly wing.
Here in my hand their hands seem to meet;
I hear in my heart the melodious beat
Of the nations that circle Divinity's feet,
As I go commonly sweeping the stair.
—Angela Morgan

March 15

Ignorant men
Don't know what good they hold in their hands until
They've flung it away.
— Sophocles

Don't it always seem to go
That you don't know what you've
got 'til it's gone
— Joni Mitchell

March 16

Death is not the enemy of life, but its friend, for it is the knowledge that our years are limited which makes them so precious. It is the truth that time is but lent to us which makes us, at our best, look upon our years as a trust handed into our temporary keeping.
— Joshua Loth Liebman

March 17

Service isn't a big thing.
It's a million little things.

I wait for a chance to confer a great favor, and let the small ones slip by; but they tell best in the end, I fancy.
— Louisa May Alcott, *Little Women*

March 18

Marriage is a sacrament instituted by God to join a man and a woman in a lifelong commitment of physical, mental, and spiritual union in their journey to God. Its purpose is twofold: First for their spiritual progress as individuals and as a couple, and for the spiritual progress of however many children they may choose to have. Second, for the preservation of the family unit as the stabilizing factor required for the physical, mental, and spiritual health of the human race.
— Jess Lair, *How to Have a Perfect Marriage*

March 19

Constant attention by a good nurse may be just as important as a major operation by a surgeon.
— Dag Hammerskjöld

When one leaf trembles, the whole bough moves.
— Chinese proverb

March 20

I am only one,
But still I am one.
I cannot do everything,
But still I can do something;
And because I cannot do everything
I will not refuse to do the something that I can do.
— Edward Everett Hale

March 21

Sow an act, and you reap a habit. Sow a habit, and you reap a character. Sow a character, and you reap a destiny.
— Charles Reade

It is from numberless diverse acts of courage and belief that human history is shaped. Each time a man stands up for an ideal, or acts to improve the lot of others, or strikes out against injustice, he sends forth a tiny ripple of hope, and crossing each other from a million different centers of energy and daring those ripples build a current which can sweep down the mightiest walls of oppression and resistance.
— Robert F. Kennedy

March 22

There is a vitality, a life-force, an energy, a quickening that is translated through you into action and because there is only one of you in all of time, this expression is unique. And if you block it, it will never exist through any other medium and be lost.
— Martha Graham

March 23

There is a desire deep within the soul which drives man from the seen to the unseen, to philosophy and to the divine.
— Kahlil Gibran

The Irresistible Intention

Spring shows
what God can do
with a drab and dirty world.
Deep in the heart of all things good
is the urge to grow and blossom.
One might as well order back the buds
as to defy the irresistible intention of man
to be better!
— Virgil A. Kraft

March 24

Once the word charity meant fellow-love;
Restore its meaning, you more fortunate;
Give us not your gold, give us yourselves instead;
Your thought, your time, your service for our need.
— Princess Amelia Rives Troubezkoy

MARCH 25

WORK WHILE YOU WORK

Work while you work,
Play while you play;
One thing each time,
That is the way.
All that you do,
Do with your might;
Things done by halves
Are not done right.

March 26

We cannot live only for ourselves. A thousand fibers connect us with our fellow man; and along these fibers, as sympathetic threads, our actions run as causes, and they come back as effects.
— Herman Melville

All the wood for a temple does not come from one tree.
— Chinese proverb

March 27

Give me such courage and I can scale
the hardest peaks alone,
And transform every stumbling block
Into a stepping stone.
— Gail Brook Burket

You can make more friends in two months by becoming interested in other people than you can in two years of trying to get other people interested in you.
— Dale Carnegie

The heavens endure; the earth is very old.
Why?
Because they do not exist for themselves, they therefore have long life.
The truly wise are content to be last; they are therefore first. They are indifferent to themselves; they are therefore self-confident.
Perhaps it is because they do not exist for themselves that they find complete fulfillment.
— *Tao*

March 29

Just as the wave cannot exist for itself, but is ever a part of the heaving surface of the ocean, so must I never live my life for itself, but always in the experience which is going on around me. It is an uncomfortable doctrine which the true ethics whisper into my ear. You are happy, they say; therefore you are called upon to give much.
— Albert Schweitzer

MARCH 30

Let me assert my firm belief that the only thing we have to fear is fear itself — nameless, unreasoning, unjustified terror which paralyzes needed efforts to convert retreat.
— Franklin D. Roosevelt

The very little engine looked up and saw the tears in the doll's eyes. . . . Then she said, "I think I can. I think I can. I think I can." She tugged and pulled and pulled and tugged and slowly, slowly they started off.
Up, up, up. Faster and faster and faster and faster the little engine climbed, until at last they reached the top of the mountain.
— Watty Piper, *The Little Engine that Could*

March 31

If you have made mistakes, even serious mistakes, there is always another chance for you. And supposing you have tried and failed again and again, you may have a fresh start any moment you choose, for this thing that we call "failure" is not the falling down, but the staying down.
— Mary Pickford

April 1

A spark of pure love is more precious before God
. . . than all the other works taken together, even
if, according to appearance, one does nothing.
— St. John of the Cross

Learn the lesson that, if you are to do the work
of a prophet, what you need is not a scepter but
a hoe.
— Bernard of Clairvaux

If you build castles in the air, your work need not
be lost; that is where they should be. Now put the
foundations under them.
— Henry David Thoreau

April 2

It is not the critic who counts; not the man who points out how the strong man stumbles, or where the doer of deeds could have done them better. The credit belongs to the man who is actually in the arena, whose face is marred by dust and sweat and blood; who strikes valiantly; who errs, and comes short again and again, because there is no effort without error and shortcoming; but who does actually strive to do the deeds, who knows the great enthusiasms, the great devotions; who spends himself in a worthy cause, who at the best knows in the end the triumph of high achievement, and who at worst, if he fails, at least fails while daring greatly, so that his place shall never be with those cold and timid souls who know neither victory nor defeat.
— Theodore Roosevelt

Things won are done, joy's soul lies in the doing.
— William Shakespeare

April 3

Settle yourself in solitude and you will come upon Him in yourself.
— Teresa of Avila

For the Great Spirit is everywhere:
He hears whatever is in our minds and hearts; it is not necessary to speak to him in a loud voice.
— Black Elk

April 4

I go through life as a transient on his way to eternity, made in the image of God but with that image debased, needing to be taught how to meditate, to worship, to think.
— Donald Coggan

"It is not enough to do, one must also become. I wish to be wiser, stronger, better. This" — I held out my hands — "this thing that is me is incomplete. It is only the raw material with which I have to work. I want to make it better than I received it."
— Louis L'Amour, *Jubal Sackett*

April 5

No horse gets anywhere till he is harnessed. No steam or gas ever drives anything until it is confined. No Niagara is ever turned into light and power until it is tunneled. No life ever grows great until it is focused, dedicated, disciplined.
—Harry Emerson Fosdick

April 6

The story of Mother Teresa's childhood and youth is, quite simply, a demonstration of how God can take the life of any individual who is willing to offer it to him, and make of it something quite literally superhuman in its power and effectiveness.
— David Porter

Oh God, you are all! Use me as you will. You made me leave the convent where I was at least of some use. Now guide me as you wish.
— Mother Teresa

April 7

No man is completely independent. Each of us is responsible to God. Many of our mental ills are due to our revolt against authority. The only way actually to be free is to submit to controls. Aristotle said, "Freedom is obedience to self-formulated rules." It would be more correct to say that freedom lies in obedience to the laws of God. Insofar as we bend our wills to the will of God, and we are responsible to Him, we are free.
— Lawrence Fitzgerald

April 8

If help and salvation are to come, they can only come from the children, for the children are the makers of men.
— Maria Montessori

Son, how can I help you see?
May I give you my shoulders to stand on?
Now you see farther than me.
Now you see for both of us.
Won't you tell me what you see?
— H. Jackson Brown, Jr.

SOMEDAY MY LOVE
Mark Ungar

Someday my love will be so great
as to dwarf these hills.
Someday my love
will pull the clouds to earth
Someday my love
will reach down to the lowest soul,
And raise him up to join me in the stars.

Someday my love will be there
when all the others have gone astray.
I'll stand on the mountain as a light for
those who wander.
Someday my love
will even pull my God to earth,
And together let us walk hand in hand.

April 10

Love is the essence of everything. Spiritual development is the ability to increase your capacity to love. If you are "soaked" in love, everything from you is dictated or governed by perfect love. Being dictated to by love is to look through the eyes of God, to take God's view, to see a person as a son or daughter of God. You want to uplift that person. You want the very best for everyone, especially those entrusted to your care.
— Paul Werner

Love, yes. This is the main word for what we need — love at all stages and with all people.
— Astrid Lindgren

April 11

There is something nobler than winning. There is something more rewarding than conquering. It is possible to be more than a conquerer. . . you had better believe that when you maintain a positive attitude in the face of persecution and persevere in doing what is right, you will be blessed.
— Robert H. Schuller, *The Be Happy Attitudes*

April 12

The prayer that reforms the sinner and heals the sick is an absolute faith that all things are possible to God.
— Mary Baker Eddy

To those who believe, no explanation is necessary; to those who do not believe, no explanation is possible.
— *The Song of Bernadette*

April 13

Saying "Yes!" to God is not a simple matter because making our lives into lives of love is not a simple or easy thing. To choose love as a life principle means that my basic mind-set or question must be: What is the loving thing to be, to do, to say? My consistent response to each of life's events, to each person who enters and touches my life, to each demand on my time and nerves and heart, must somehow be transformed into an act of love. However, in the last analysis, it is this "Yes!" that opens me to God. Choosing love as a life principle widens the chalice of my soul, so that God can pour into me his gifts and graces and powers.
— John Powell, S. J., *Unconditional Love*

April 14

We've gotten to the point where everybody's got a right and nobody's got a responsibility. I suppose that's the ultimate result of our society being afraid to distinguish between right and wrong.
— Newton Minow

A man's worst difficulties begin when he is able to do as he likes.
— Thomas Henry Huxley

April 15

All the world's religions come out against unmitigated selfishness. That's a common ethos.
— Kenneth Boulding

The answer does not lie there, but in the hearts of men, in the quiet revolution from selfishness to unselfishness.
Can you imagine how wonderful the ideal society will be? Individuals will belong to their families, the family will belong to the society, the society will belong to the nation, the nation will belong to the world, the world will belong to God, and God will belong to you.
— Sun Myung Moon

April 16

It is not in the still calm of life, or the repose of a pacific station, that great characters are formed. . . . The habits of a vigorous mind are formed in contending with difficulties. All history will convince you of this, and that wisdom and penetration are the fruit of experience, not the lessons of retirement and leisure. Great necessities call out great virtues.
— Abigail Adams

April 17

The beginning of turning things around so that the species can survive is to be found precisely in the search for universal values. We must take it much more seriously than we do.
— A. H. Halsey

I am personally convinced that there are certain absolute norms that can be rendered to be sufficiently applicable for certain situations. You should be able, no matter what background you come from, to arrive at certain absolute laws.
— Bernard Przewozny

April 18

Drop a pebble in the water
And its ripples reach out far;
And the sunbeams dancing on them
May reflect them to a star.

Give a smile to someone passing,
Thereby make his morning glad;
It will greet you in the evening
When your own heart may be sad.

Do a deed of simple kindness;
Though its end you may not see,
It may reach, like widening ripples,
Down a long eternity.
—James W. Fowley

We do not need more material development; we need more spiritual development . . . we do not need more law; we need more religion. We do not need more of the things that are seen; we need more of the things that are unseen.
— Calvin Coolidge

April 20

The basic fact of today is the tremendous pace of change in human life. In my own life I have seen amazing changes, and I am sure that in the course of the life of the next generation these changes will be even greater . . . nothing is so remarkable as the progressive conquest of understanding of the physical world by the mind of man today. While there has been this conquest of external conditions, there is at the same time the strange spectacle of a lack of moral fiber and of self-control in man as a whole. Conquering the physical world, he fails to conquer himself.
— Jawaharlal Nehru, *The New Leader*

I have more trouble with myself than with any other man.
— Dwight L. Moody

April 21

Everybody thinks of changing humanity and nobody thinks of changing himself.
— Tolstoy

Lord, make this a better world — beginning with me!
— Claire MacMurray

April 22

Prayer is a force as real as terrestrial gravity. As a physician, I have seen men, after all other therapy had failed, lifted out of disease and melancholy by the serene effort of prayer. It is the only power in the world that seems to overcome the so-called "laws of nature;" the occasions on which prayer had dramatically done this have been termed "miracles." But a constant, quieter miracle takes place hourly in the hearts of men and women who have discovered that prayer supplies them with a steady flow of sustaining power in their lives.
— Alexis Carrel

April 23

If you think the world is all wrong, remember that it contains people like you.
— Mohandas K. Gandhi

The most ignorant among mankind have some truth in them. We are all sparks of truth.
— Mohandas K. Gandhi

April 24

To do something better, you must work an extra bit harder. I like the phrase an extra bit harder. For me this is not just a slogan, but a habitual state of mind, a disposition. Any job one takes on must be grasped and felt with one's soul, mind and heart; only then will one work an extra bit harder.
— Mikhail Gorbachev

April 25

One only gets to the top rung on the ladder by steadily climbing up one at a time, and suddenly all sorts of powers, all sorts of abilities which you thought never belonged to you — suddenly become within your possibility, and you think, "Well, I'll have a go, too."
— Margaret Thatcher

April 26

Develop a train of thought on which to ride. The nobility of your life as well as your happiness depends upon the direction in which that chain of thought is going.
— Dr. Laurence J. Peter

All that we are is the result of what we thought.
— Buddha

Without sacrifice there is no resurrection. Nothing grows and blooms save by giving. All you try to save in yourself wastes and perishes. How do you know the fruit is ripe? Because it leaves the bough. All things ripen for giving's sake and in the giving are consummated.
— André Gide

April 28

It's important that people know what you stand for. It's equally important that they know what you won't stand for.
— Mary Waldrop

If we don't stand for something, we will fall for nothing.
— Irene Dunne

April 29

Spirituality leads us to service and solitude. We care for our fellows and take action to show it. We have a love for ourselves. We care for our own life. We love others as an expansion of our own life. We understand that by giving we receive. We grasp that by lighting other's candles, we do not lose our own light. The more candles one lights, the more enlightened the world becomes.
— John Bradshaw, *Creating Love*

April 30

If we are:
too busy to read a book that promises to widen our horizons;
too busy to keep our friendships in good repair;
too busy to maintain a consistent devotional life;
too busy to keep the warm vital loves of our home burning;
too busy to conserve our health in the interest of our highest efficiency;
too busy to spend one hour during the week in church;
too busy to cultivate our own souls;
then we are indeed
TOO BUSY!
— Pat Barlow

For fast-acting relief, try slowing down.
— Lily Tomlin

May 1

Far away there in the sunshine are my highest aspirations. I may not reach them but I can look up and see their beauty, believe in them and try to follow them.
— Louisa May Alcott

The most pathetic person in the world is someone who has sight, but has no vision.
— Helen Keller

May 2

As long as men are inwardly in conflict, divided within themselves, victims of their own inner opposition, they are easy prey to evil. But where the kingdom of God is being established in an individual, he is also becoming whole and the kingdom of evil has no power over him.
— John Sanford, *The Kingdom Within*

May 3

The best index to a person's character is (a) how he treats people who can't do him any good, and (b) how he treats people who can't fight back.
— Abigail Van Buren

The chief lesson I have learned in a long life is that the only way to make a man trustworthy is to trust him; and the surest way to make him untrustworthy is to distrust him and show your mistrust.
— Henry L. Stimson

May 4

Who can order the Holy? It is like a rain forest, dripping, lush, fecund, wild. We enter its abundance at our peril, for here we are called to the wholesome for which we long, but which requires all we are and can hope to be.
— Marilyn Sewell, *Cries of the Spirit*

One must not stand up and say the tefillah except in a serious frame of mind. The pious men of old used to wait for an hour, and then say the prayer, in order to direct their hearts to their Father in heaven.
— Mishnah, Berakot 5.1

MAY 5

Parents are the source of love for the family. The original nature of parental love is to give unconditionally, without any reservation; such love nurtures children's physical and spiritual development. Through their parents' love children experience God's heart and love, receiving nourishment, shelter, protection, guidance, discipline, and all the many facets of parental love. Parental love is the heartbeat of the family, transmitting life-giving elements to the children's spirit. God, our heavenly parent, is the heart and source of parental love; thus He should be the core of the family.
— Joong Hyun Pak, *Joymakers*

May 6

Beyond Perls
Walter Tubbs

If I just do my thing and you do yours,
We stand in danger of losing each other
And ourselves.
I am not in this world to live up to your expectations;
But I am in this world to confirm you
As a unique human being.
And to be confirmed by you.

We are fully ourselves only in relation to each other;
The I detached from a Thou
Disintegrates.

I do not find you by chance;
I find you by an active life
Of reaching out.

Rather than passively letting things happen to me,
I can act intentionally to make them happen.

I must begin with myself, true;
But I must not end with myself:
The truth begins with two.

MAY 7

Moral virtue is not learnt in schools. If good moral habits are acquired at all, they are ordinarily within the family, within the neighborhood, within the circle of close associates in youth; often good moral habits, or bad ones, are fixed by the age of seven, little more than a year after school has begun for the child. The early life of the household and the early life of the streets counts for immensely much.
— Russell Kirk

Children have never been very good at listening to their elders, but they have never failed to imitate them.
— James Baldwin, *Nobody Knows My Name*

May 8

To have faith requires courage, the ability to take a risk, the readiness even to accept pain and disappointment. Whoever insists on safety and security as primary conditions of life cannot have faith; whoever shuts himself off in a system of defense, where distance and possession are his means of security, makes him a prisoner. To be loved, and to love, need courage, the courage to judge certain values as of ultimate concern — and to take the jump and stake everything on these values.
— Erich Fromm

MAY 9

Fortunately analysis is not the only way to resolve inner conflicts. Life itself still remains a very effective therapist.
— Karen Horney

It has often been noted that most, if not all, problems brought to therapists are issues of love. It makes sense that the cure is also love.
— Thomas Moore

MAY 10

THE SECRETS

- Love has only one sure route: unconditional support, even if you're scared, even if you have to bluff it.
- We become what we name each other. Call me rascal and watch how cute and rascally I get. Call me stubborn and watch.
- Speak your love out loud. Saying it often — saying it enough — makes it invincible.
- Dependency is not a dirty word. Risking reliance on another can be the way to self-growth.
- Home is safe harbor for all the family — even if they kick up a storm there.
- A good laugh tames a tempest. If you're not funny, get funny.
- Spend time together: hearing about catching the shark isn't the same as feeling shark's breath.
- Only when you let yourself be completely vulnerable will the earth move.
- Just when you think you know everything there is to know about him, there's another layer revealed. If you dig.
- Lying, even a little, puts you in treacherous water; getting your bearings in marriage requires honesty in the small things.

— Sherry Suib Cohen,
Secrets of a Very Good Marriage

May 11

She did not talk to people as if they were strange hard shells she had to crack open to get inside. She talked as if she were already in the shell. In their very shell.
— Marita Bonner, *Frye Street and Environs*

Oh, the comfort, the inexpressible comfort of feeling safe with a person; having neither to weigh thoughts nor to measure words but to pour them all out, just as it is, chaff and grain together, knowing that a faithful hand will take and sift them, keeping what is worth keeping, and then, with the breath of kindness, blow the rest away.
— George Eliot

May 12

To receive a present handsomely and in the right spirit, even when you have none to give in return, is to give one in return.
— Leigh Hunt

He that gives me small gifts would have me live.
— English proverb

To give quickly is a great virtue.
— Hindu proverb

May 13

If you promise pie in the sky, that's hard to check up on. But if you promise pie for the grandchildren, and the grandchildren turn up and there's no pie, the whole thing's over.
— Kenneth Boulding

Make no mistake about it, responsibility toward other human beings are the greatest blessings God sent us.
— Dorothy Dix

May 14

Iniquity, committed in this world, produces not fruit immediately, but, like the earth, in due season, and advancing little by little, it eradicates the man who committed it.

He grows rich for a while through unrighteousness; then he beholds good things; then it is that he vanquishes his foes; but he perishes at length from his whole root upwards.

Justice, being destroyed, will destroy; being preserved, will preserve; it must never therefore be violated.

— Manu, c. 1200 B.C.

MAY 15

Two friends playing together. And love is when you like to play when he wants to and you may not want to.
— David Wilson, age 7

Who seeks a faultless friend remains friendless.
— Turkish proverb

May 16

A traveler heading for Smithville came to a fork in the road where the arm of a signpost reading "five miles to Smithville" pointed up a steep, rocky hill. The other fork led down a delightful, tree-lined road, running beside a cool, babbling brook. It seemed sensible to him at the moment to climb up and change the sign around, so that the Smithville marker pointed down the comfortable path. The traveler walked and walked, but he never got to Smithville.

Before you begin a thing remind yourself that difficulties and delays quite impossible to foresee are ahead. If you could see them clearly, naturally you could do a great deal to get rid of them but you can't. You can only see one thing clearly and that is your goal. Form a mental vision of that and cling to it through thick and thin.
— Kathleen Norris, *Hands Full of Living*

The man who gives up accomplishes nothing and is only a hindrance. The man who does not give up can move mountains.
— Ernest Hello, *Life, Science, and Art*

May 18

God's love is true, selfless and unchanging. True love is the act of giving without the condition of receiving. When God created us, He invested one hundred percent of everything He had again and again. The reason why God wanted to invest Himself completely is because He wanted His object of love to be better than Himself. The act of living for others means that you give one hundred percent of yourself until there is nothing left to give. Only then will the love of your object rush back to fill the void. An example of this is the earth's atmosphere. When a low pressure system forms, air moves in from a high pressure system. The air starts circulating, and can even result in a hurricane. In other words, it is the complete rendering and sacrificing of yourself for the sake of others that produces a vacuum, which will be the very source of tremendous power when God replenishes you with His love.

God's true love is such that though He loves and loves again, or gives and gives again, He does so unconditionally and unconsciously. If you consciously remember what you have given, then you will begin to calculate how much giving is enough. And if you decide that you have given enough, then love cannot continue eternally. Love flows perpetually only if it is given unconditionally.

— Hak Ja Han Moon

May 19

How to hit home runs: I swing as hard as I can, and I try to swing right thru the ball, I swing big, with everything I've got. I hit big or I miss big. I like to live as big as I can.
— Babe Ruth

A life is not important, except in the impact it has on other lives.
— Jackie Robinson

Jimmy: Quitting — You'll regret it for the rest of your life. Baseball is what gets inside you . . .
Dotty: It just got too hard.
Jimmy: It's supposed to be hard. If it wasn't hard everyone would do it. The hard is what makes it great.
— *A League of Their Own*

May 20

Words of truth are not high-sounding; high-sounding words are not truth. One who has Teh does not argue; so one who argues does not have Teh. The truly wise do not know many things; one who knows many things is not truly wise. The truly wise do not selfishly crave. They live for other people and thereby grow richer. They give freely of themselves and thereby have great abundance. The great Tao endows but does so unconditionally. The Tao of the wise accomplishes but does so unselfishly.

— *Tao*

Prayer, like radium, is a source of luminous energy, and when we pray we link ourselves with the inexhaustible motive power that spins the universe.
— Alexis Carrel

Prayer is not hearing yourself talk, but being silent, staying silent, and waiting until you hear God.
— Søren Kierkegaard

May 22

Congregations are strange, wonderful, and unique communities.... What other communities are constituted as ecologies of vocation, where people call forth and confirm each other's gifts and giftedness for the service of God, and support and hold each other accountable in the use of these gifts? Where else will you encounter the generativity and generosity that characterize congregational life at its best — a generosity that has gratitude to God as its motive and approaches investment in others as an opportunity to return something of what one has been graciously given by others? In what other community do people work at seeing each other whole, offsetting the societal reduction of the person to customer, client, patient, student, boss or employee, or sucker in the marketplace?
— James M. Fowler, *Weaving the New Creation*

May 23

I was sitting, torn by grief. Someone came and talked to me of God's dealings, of why it happened, [the death of one of his three children] of hope beyond the grave. He talked constantly. He said things I knew were true.

I was unmoved, except to wish he'd go away. He finally did.

Another came and sat beside me. He didn't talk. He didn't ask me leading questions. He just sat beside me for an hour and more, listening when I said something, answered briefly, prayed simply, left.

I was moved. I was comforted. I hated to see him go.

— Joe Bayly, *The Last Things We Talk About*

May 24

Tell me not in mournful numbers,
Life is but an empty dream!
Lives of great men all remind us
We can make our lives sublime,
And, departing, leave behind us
Footprints on the sands of time.
— Henry Wadsworth Longfellow

MAY 25

Your vision will become clear only when you can look into your own heart. Who looks outside, dreams; who looks inside, awakes.
— Carl G. Jung

"The men where you live," said the little prince, "raise five thousand roses in the same garden — and they do not find in it what they are looking for. And yet what they are looking for could be found in one single rose or in a little water. But the eyes are blind. One must look with the heart."
— Antoine de St.-Exupery, *The Little Prince*

May 26

There is not a single saint who sits in a single church free from a few things he or she is ashamed of — not one of us! The one who thinks otherwise is worse than all the rest combined.

Mark it — when God forgives, He forgets. He is not only willing but pleased to use any vessel — just as long as it is clean today. It may be cracked or chipped. It may be worn or it may have never been used before. You can count on this — the past ended one second ago. From this point onward, you can be clean. . . . God's glorious grace says: "Throw guilt and anxiety overboard . . . draw the anchor . . . trim the sails . . . man the rudder . . . a strong gale is coming!"

— Charles Swindoll,
Growing Strong in the Seasons of Life

In Flanders Fields
John McCrae

In Flanders fields the poppies blow
Between the crosses, row on row,
That mark our place; and in the sky
The larks, still bravely singing, fly
Scarce heard amid the guns below.

We are the Dead. Short days ago
We lived, felt dawn, saw sunset glow,
Loved and were loved, and now we lie
In Flanders fields.

Take up our quarrel with the foe;
To you from failing hands we throw
The torch; be yours to hold it high.
If ye break faith with us who die
We shall not sleep, though poppies grow
In Flanders fields.

May 28

If you can talk with crowds and keep your virtue,
Or walk with kings—nor lose the common touch;
If neither foes nor loving friends can hurt you;
If all men count with you, but none too much;
If you can fill the unforgiving minute
With sixty seconds' worth of distance run—
Yours is the Earth and everything that's in it,
And — which is more — you'll be a man, my son!
— Rudyard Kipling, *If—*

MAY 29

I do not believe that we are all created equal. Physical and emotional differences, parental guidance, varying environments, being in the right place at the right time all play a role in enhancing or limiting development. But I do believe every man or woman, if given the opportunity and encouragement to recognize his or her potential, regardless of background, has the freedom to choose in our world. Will an individual be a taker or a giver in life? Will he be satisifed merely to exist or will he seek a meaningful purpose?

I believe every person is created as the steward of his or her own destiny with great power for a specific purpose to share with others, through service, a reverence for life in a spirit of love.

— Robert H. Schuller, *The Be Happy Attitudes*

May 30

Every generation feels the impulse of hope. Every generation so far has had that impulse crushed. What we want to do is to recreate innocence in a world of experience. We want to embrace the world as it is, not to curse it, but to bless it. That is our hope for the future. We want to bring forth light from where there is darkness, to work rather than sit still lamenting the fate of the world. That is our great task, our great mission, and our great challenge as a people throughout the world. For, after all, when all the churches are forgotten, there is only one human family, if we can make it a family.

— Mose Durst, To Bigotry, No Sanction

MAY 31

Some day, after we have mastered the winds, the waves, the tides and gravity, we will harness for God the energies of love and then for the second time in the history of the world man will have discovered fire.
— Pierre Teilhard de Chardin

June 1

To be courageous . . . requires no exceptional qualifications, no magic formula, no special combination of time, place and circumstance. It is an opportunity that sooner or later is presented to us all. Politics merely furnishes one arena which imposes special tests of courage. In whatever arena of life one may meet the challenge of courage, whatever may be the sacrifices he faces if he follows his conscience — the loss of his friends, his fortune, his contentment, even the esteem of his fellow men — each man must decide for himself the course he will follow. The stories of past courage can define that ingredient — they can teach, they can offer hope, they can provide inspiration. But they cannot supply courage itself. For this each man must look into his own soul.
— John F. Kennedy, *Profiles in Courage*

June 2

What am I doing here? I'm here to serve mankind — it doesn't matter what I "do."
— Le Ly Hayslip

Past the seeker as he prayed, came the crippled and the beggar and the beaten. And seeing them, the holy one went down into deep prayer and cried, "Great God, how is it that a loving creator can see such things and yet do nothing about them?"
"I did do something. I made you."
— Sufi teaching story

June 3

If you hear that someone is speaking ill of you, instead of trying to defend yourself you should say: "He obviously does not know me very well, since there are so many other faults he could have mentioned."
— Epictetus, *Enchiridion*

The test of good manners is to be patient with bad ones.
— Solomon Ibn Gabriol, *The Choice of Pearls*

June 4

The greatest and most lasting impression made upon me at Hampton was that made by General Armstrong, the noblest, rarest human being I have ever met. The older I grow, the more I am convinced that there is no education one can get from books and costly apparatus that is equal to that which can be gotten from contact with great men and women. From his example I learned the lesson that great men cultivate love, and that only little men cherish a spirit of hatred.
— Booker T. Washington

June 5

Let the disciple cultivate love without measure toward all beings.
Let him cultivate love toward the whole world, above, below, a heart of love unstinted . . .
For in all the world this state of heart is best.
— Buddha

A new commandment I give to you, that you love one another.
— Jesus

June 6

During our journey there were two occasions that we celebrated by honoring someone's talent. Everyone is recognized by a special party, but it has nothing to do with age or birthdate — it is in recognition of uniqueness and contribution to life. They believe that the purpose for the passage of time is to allow a person to become better, wiser, to express more and more of one's beingness. So if you are a better person this year than last, and only you know that for certain, then you call for the party. When you say you are ready, everyone honors that.
— Marlo Morgan, *Mutant Message*

June 7

The best way to know God is to love many things.
— Vincent Van Gogh

Express your ultimate concern for whatever is before you.
Hug your daughter as if she is all the humanity that will follow after you. Caress your lover as if his is the body of God. Hug your dog as if it is all life in the universe and scrub the floor as if it is a sacred offering to your family and the world.
— Frank Andrews

June 8

Who is wise? He who learns from all men.
— Talmud

I believe in person to person; every person is Christ for me, and since there is only one Jesus, that person is the one person in the world at that moment.
— Mother Teresa

June 9

I suppose the simplest explanation for the great popularity of Mother Teresa is that, in a world of structures and technology in which no person seems to matter very much, she has affirmed the preciousness of each human life.
— Abigail McCarthy

The effect of one upright individual is incalculable.
— Oscar Arias

JUNE 10

Ask yourself and yourself alone, this one question — does this path have a heart. If it does the path is good, if it does not, it is of no use.
— Don Juan (Carlos Castaneda)

Where love is what can be wanting? Where it is not, what can possibly be profitable?
— St. Augustine

Love doesn't make the world go 'round. Love is what makes the ride worthwhile.
— Franklin P. Jones

June 11

There are no ordinary people. You have never talked to a mere mortal. Nations, cultures, arts, civilizations— these are mortal, and their life is to ours as the life of a gnat. But it is immortals whom we joke with, work with, marry, snub, and exploit — immortal horrors or everlasting splendors. This does not mean that we are to be perpetually solemn. We must play. But our merriment must be of that kind (and it is, in fact, the merriest kind) — which exists between people who have, from the outset, taken each other seriously — no flippancy, no superiority, no presumption.
— C. S. Lewis, *The Weight of Glory*

June 12

Worry a little bit every day and in a lifetime you will lose a couple of years. If something is wrong, fix it if you can. But train yourself not to worry. Worry never fixes anything.
— Mary Hemingway

I think that these difficult times have helped me to understand better than before how infinitely rich and beautiful life is in every way and that so many things that one goes around worrying about are of no importance whatsoever.
— Isak Dinesen

June 13

Heaven Is Not Reached in a Single Bound
J. G. Holland

Heaven is not reached in a single bound,
But we build the ladder by which we rise
From the lowly earth to the vaulted skies,
And we mount to its summit round by round.

I count this thing to be grandly true:
That a noble deed is a step toward God —
Lifting the soul from the common clod
To a purer air and a broader view.

June 14

The brave man is not he who feels no fear,
For that were stupid and irrational;
But he whose noble soul its fears subdues,
And bravely dares the danger nature shrinks from.
— Joanna Baille

Bravery is being the only one who knows you're afraid.
— Franklin P. Jones

June 15

The family has always been the cornerstone of American society.

Our families nurture, preserve and pass on to each succeeding generation the values we share and cherish, values that are the foundation for our freedoms. In the family, we learn our first lessons of God and man, love and discipline, rights and responsibilities, human dignity and human frailty. Our families give us daily examples of these lessons being put into practice. In raising and instructing our children, in providing personal and compassionate care for the elderly, in maintaining the spiritual strength of religious commitment among our people — in these and other ways, America's families make immeasurable contributions to America's well-being.

Today more than ever, it is essential that these contributions not be taken for granted and that each of us remember that the strength of our families is vital to the strength of our nation.

— Ronald Reagan

June 16

He's a man out there in the blue, rid'n on a smile and a shoeshine . . . a salesman has got to dream, boys.
— Arthur Miller

We have always held to the hope, the belief, the conviction that there is a better life, a better world, beyond the horizon.
— Franklin D. Roosevelt

June 17

Each person has inside a basic decency and goodness. If he listens to it and acts on it, he is giving a great deal of what it is the world needs most. It is not complicated but it takes courage. It takes courage for a person to listen to his own goodness and act on it.
— Pablo Casals

June 18

Spiritual rose bushes are not like natural rose bushes; with these latter the thorns remain but the roses pass, with the former the thorns pass and the roses remain.
— St. Francis De Sales

I forgot that every little action of the common day makes or unmakes character, and that therefore what one has done in the secret chamber one has some day to cry aloud on the house-tops.
— Oscar Wilde, *De Profundis*

June 19

A professor was invited to speak at a military base and was met at the airport by an unforgettable soldier named Ralph. As they headed toward the baggage claim area, Ralph kept disappearing; once to help an older woman with her suitcase; once to lift two toddlers so they could see Santa Claus; and again to give someone directions. Each time he came back smiling.

"Where did you learn to live like that?" the professor asked.

"During the war," said Ralph. Then he told the professor about Vietnam. His job was to clear minefields, and he saw friends meet untimely ends, one after another, before his eyes.

"I learned to live between steps," he said. "I never knew whether the next one would be my last, so I had to get everything I could out of that moment between picking up my foot and putting it down again. Every step felt like a whole new world."

— *Leadership*

June 20

Spread your thoughts of love beyond limits.
— Buddha

If I speak in the tongues of men and angels but have not love, I am a noisy gong or clanging cymbal. And if I have prophetic powers and understand all mysteries and all knowledge and if I have all faith, so as to move mountains, but do not have love, I am nothing.
— St. Paul

June 21

A little girl in a migrant camp fell in love with one of the dolls in the toy box, but she had to put it back when play time was over.

At Christmas time the camp staff arranged to give toys and agreed to let the child with perfect attendance have first choice. A beautiful doll was placed in the center of the gifts and the little girl having had perfect attendance was permitted to choose first. Her eyes nearly popped as she stood rigid before the doll. She stared in wonder, then she turned and took a tricycle.

When asked why, she said her little brother had wanted a bike and now she could give him one.

— Dean Collins

June 22

No life is so hard that you can't make it easier by the way you take it.
— Ellen Glasgow

I discovered I always have choices and sometimes it's only a choice of attitude.
— Judith M. Knowlton

June 23

Most important, we must return religion to its proper place. Religion provides us with moral bearings, and the solution to our chief problem of spiritual impoverishment depends on spiritual renewal, the surrendering of strong beliefs, in our private moralized society.

Today we must carry on a new struggle for the country we love. We must push hard against an age that is pushing hard against us. If we have full employment and greater economic growth — if we have cities of gold and alabaster — but our children have not learned how to walk in goodness, justice and mercy, then the American experiment, no matter how gilded, will have failed. Do not surrender. Get mad. Get in the fight.

— William J. Bennett

JUNE 24

Like anybody, I would like to live a long life. Longevity has its place. But I'm not concerned about that now. I just want to do God's will. And He's allowed me to go up to the mountain. And I've looked over, and I've seen the promised land. I may not get there with you, but I want you to know tonight that we as a people will get to the promised land.
— Martin Luther King, April 5, 1968
(the day before his assassination)

> Free at last, free at last
> Thank God almighty
> We are free at last
> — Martin Luther King during the march on Washington, August, 1963

June 25

To have friends whose lives we can elevate or depress by our influence is sacred. To be entrusted with little children is sacred. To have powers by which we can make this earth a more decent place is sacred. To be a child of God is sacred. And honor, honesty, truthfulness, fidelity, and love are sacred.
— Harry Emerson Fosdick

All the people of the whole world are equally brothers and sisters. There is no one who is an utter stranger. There is no one who has known the truth of this origin. It is the very cause of the regret of God. The souls of all people are equal, whether they live on the high mountains or at the bottoms of the valleys.
— Ofudesaki 13.43–45

What is the true color of love? Black? White? True love has no color. Anyone who is color-conscious cannot have true love at all. You have got to be color-blind.
— Sun Myung Moon

June 27

There are times when our children, perhaps unconsciously, see into the heart of life, after the fashion of the little girl who remarked, "Mother, I've had such a happy time today." "Really," her mother answered. "What made today different from yesterday?" The child thought a moment and them responded, "Yesterday my thoughts pushed me around and today I pushed my thoughts around."

Those perceptive words of a child picture life as it is, a perpetual struggle between the things that push us around and the inner resources that enable us to push our lives where they ought to go.

— Harold Blake Walker

June 28

When all human beings have accomplished the purification of their minds and come to lead a life full of joy, I, Tsukihi [God], will become cheered up. And when I become cheered up, so will all human beings. When the minds of all the world become cheered up, God and human beings will become altogether cheered up in one accord.
— Ofudesaki 7.109–11

God has promised to believers . . . beautiful mansions in Gardens of everlasting bliss. But the greatest bliss is the good pleasure of God: that is the supreme felicity.
— Qur'an 9.72

Cowles was a little lad. One day he tried something on the mantel and found it was beyond him. He came down from stretching on tiptoe and said to his mother, "I am not very big, am I, Mama? I can't reach very high." His mother reached out, as she noted the serious look on his face, and said to him, "No, you are not very big now, my son, but you will grow and some day you will be a big man like your papa." He stood erect as the faith within him spoke, "Mama, I feel a man pushing inside of me now!"
— Katherine Logan, *There's Something Better*

June 30

Rabbi Eliezer ben Jacob says, "He who carries out one good deed acquires one advocate in his own behalf, and he who commits one transgression acquires one accuser against himself. Repentance and good works are like a shield against calamity."
— Mishnah, Abot 4.13

Your luck is how you treat people.
— Bridget O'Donnell

JULY 1

There is a story that one night in 1945, General Dwight Eisenhower walked along the Rhine, thinking of the crossing in which he would lead the Allied armies. He met a soldier and asked him why he wasn't sleeping. The young G.I. didn't recognize the Supreme Commander. "I guess I'm a little nervous," he said. "Well, so am I," said Eisenhower. "Let's walk together and perhaps we'll draw strength from each other."
— James A. Reiner

No matter what accomplishments you achieve, somebody helps you.
— Althea Gibson

July 2

Who are the great inventors of the world? . . . The great inventor sits next to you, or you are the person yourself. "Oh," but you will say, "I have never invented anything in my life." Neither did the great inventors until they discovered one great secret. Do you think it is a man with a head like a bushel measure or a man like a stroke of lightning? It is neither. The really great man is a plain, straightforward, everyday, common-sense man. You would not dream that he was a great inventor if you did not see something he had actually done. His neighbors do not regard him as great. You never see anything great over your back fence. You say there is no greatness among your neighbors. It is all away off somewhere else. Their greatness is ever so simple, so plain, so earnest, so practical that the neighbors and friends never recognize it.

— Russell H. Conwell, *Acres of Diamonds*

July 3

The Body Is A Jewel

What diamonds are equal to my eyes?
What labyrinths to my ears?
What gates of ivory or ruby leaves to the
double portal of my lips and teeth?
Is not sight a jewel?
Is not hearing a treasure?
Is not speech a glory?

O my Lord, pardon my ingratitude, and pity my dullness who am not sensible of these gifts.
The freedom of Thou bounty hath deceived me
These things were too near to be considered.
Thou presenteth me with Thy blessings, and I was not aware.
But now I give thanks and adore and praise Thee for Thine inestimable favors.
— Thomas Traherne, 1637–1674

July 4

No matter how wealthy and famous you may be, unless you have someone with whom to have give and take so that you can share your joy, your sorrow, your opinions, and your ideals, you are just a poor man.
— *God's Hope for Man*

When love beckons to you, follow him, though his ways are hard and steep.
— Kahlil Gibran

July 5

My motto is, "Even though I cannot do it, I will try my best; even though I cannot do it perfectly, I will still take up the challenge."
— Haruko Kanari

I have resolved to run when I can, to go when I cannot run, and to creep when I cannot go. As to the main, I thank Him who loved me, I am fixed; my way is before me, my mind is beyond the River that has no bridge.
— John Bunyan, 1628–1688

July 6

I stand before the map of the world; before its countries stretched wide and its waters deep. I stand before the rivers lying like long crooked fingers across the land, fed forever from the streams, the snows and the rains of the mountains, pouring endlessly into the seas.

Up and down the rivers people have their mansions and the squatted huts. Children are born, and families fish the waters for food, or till the soil of the valleys and countrysides. Some families work in the factories and some in the dark interior of the earth.

How alike we are around the world; living in our families, working and playing, having fun and having sorrow, knowing fear and security, needing food and clothing.

On this day I send into families of the world my wishes for good will. I will make room in my heart for all my brothers and sisters everywhere.
— Abbie Graham

Father, enlarge my sympathies. Give me a roomier heart! May my life be like a great hospitable tree, and may weary wanderers find in me a rest.
— John Henry Jowett

JULY 7

John Wesley's mother taught her son, "Whatever weakens your reason, impairs the tenderness of your conscience, obscures your sense of God, takes off your relish for spiritual things, whatever increases the authority of the body over the mind, that thing is sin to you, however innocent it may seem in itself."
— Stephen R. Covey,
Principle-Centered Leadership

July 8

There is a certain relief in change, even though it ebb from bad to worse; as I have found in traveling in a stagecoach, that it is often a comfort to shift one's position and be bounced in a new place.
— Washington Irving

Change is the constant, the signal for rebirth, the egg of the phoenix.
— Christina Baldwin, *One to One*

July 9

What do we do with our anger when we have been hurt? The goal, if we can achieve it, would be to be angry at the situation, rather than at ourselves, or at those who might have prevented it or are close to us trying to help us, or at God who let it happen. Getting angry at ourselves makes us depressed. Being angry at other people scares them away and makes it harder for them to help us. Being angry at God erects a barrier between us and all the sustaining, comforting resources of religion that are there to help us at such times. But being angry at the situation, recognizing it as something rotten, unfair, and totally undeserved, shouting about it, denouncing it, crying over it, permits us to discharge the anger which is a part of being hurt, without making it harder for us to be helped.
— Harold S. Kushner,
When Bad Things Happen to Good People

July 10

Blessed are those who can give without remembering, and take without forgetting.
— Elizabeth Bibesco, *Balloons*

A cheerful giver does not count the cost of what he gives. His heart is set on pleasing and cheering him to whom the gift is given.
— Julian of Norwich,
Revelations of Divine Love, 1373

July 11

Once there was a young woman named Kisagotami, the wife of a wealthy man, who lost her mind because of the death of her child. She took the dead child in her arms and went from house to house begging people to heal the child. Of course, they could do nothing for her, but finally a follower of Buddha advised her to see the Blessed One.

He looked upon her with sympathy and said: "To heal the child I need some poppy seeds; go and beg four or five poppy seeds from some home where death has never entered."

So the demented woman went out and sought a house where death had never entered, but in vain. At last, she was obliged to return to Buddha. In his quiet presence her mind cleared and she understood the meaning of his words. She took the body away and buried it, and then returned to Buddha and became one of his followers.

— *The Teaching of Buddha*

July 12

There is nothing more lovely in life than the union of two people whose love for one another has grown through the years from the small acorn of passion to a great rooted tree. Surviving all vicissitudes, and rich with its manifold branches, every leaf holding its own significance.
— Vita Sackville-West, *No Signposts in the Sea*

A good marriage is one which allows for change and growth in the individuals and in the way they express their love.
— Pearl S. Buck, *To My Daughters, With Love*

July 13

A Child's Prayer
M. Bentham-Edwards

God make my life a little light,
Within the world to glow;
A tiny flame that burneth bright
Wherever I may go.

God make my life a little flower,
That giveth joy to all,
Content to bloom in native bower,
Although its place be small.

God make my life a little song,
That comforteth the sad;
That helpeth others to be strong,
And makes the singer glad.

God make my life a little staff,
Whereon the weak may rest,
That so what health and strength I have
May serve my neighbors best.

July 14

We have love and life, we need one thing further — an ideal. These three elements — love, life and an ideal — are not just precious and profound in value, they are the very things that make our lives worth living.
— *God's Hope for Man*

One needs something to believe in, something for which one can have whole-hearted enthusiasm. One needs to feel that one's life has meaning, that one is needed in this world.
— Hannah Senesh

July 15

"As your father cleans his lamps to have good light, so keep clean your spirit."
"And how shall it be kept clean, Mr. Gruffydd?" I asked him.
"By prayer, my son," he said, "not mumbling, or shouting, or wallowing like a hog in religious sentiments. Prayer is only another name for good, clean, direct thinking. When you pray, think well what you are saying, and make your thoughts into things that are solid. In that manner, your prayer will have strength, and that strength shall become part of you, mind, body and spirit."
— Richard Llewellyn, *How Green Was My Valley*

July 16

We will give it unto our children, and they unto their children, and it shall not perish.
— Kahlil Gibran

The greatest Glory of a free-born People,
Is to transmit that Freedom to their Children.
— William Havard, *Regulus, a Tragedy*

July 17

How does the family synthesize the facts of human relatedness and responsibility? As individuals, we live and grow in the matrix of a family. Our parents teach us what it means to be worthwhile persons. We grow in wisdom and stature under guidance. From them we learn how to love and respond. Therefore, the responses we make to our family environment have a decisive impact upon the personal maturation of our children. "Like father, like son" or "Like mother, like daughter," we say. When parents live according to God's standard, their children will respect, obey them and follow their example. God originates the family structure, making it an instrument for the realization of His parental love and authority. But nearly as important are the responses we make to our fathers, mothers, brothers, sisters and children. Only if these kinship relationships are positive and creative is it possible to manifest the full give and take of love with God and our fellow man.

— Young Oon Kim

July 18

If we could read the secret history of our enemies, we should find in each man's life sorrow and suffering enough to disarm all hostility.
— Henry Wadsworth Longfellow

Compassion is a way to interpret someone. With compassion you see a person's behavior against the broader plight in which he or she lives.
— Frank Andrews

July 19

We fail to realize, as we encounter the frustrations of loving, that love is not necessarily a momentary emotional high that takes away the feeling of emptiness. Love, rather, is the disciplined process of mind, emotion and will in which we create consistency, stability and strength in relationship focused on purpose. Like a great work of art, a human life of beauty is built over time through consistent, purposeful, virtuous action. We need not be too frightened by our feeling of inadequacy because in many ways we are inadequate before we become adequate. Immaturity must be the stage which precedes maturity. Our chief concern should be the direction of our growth.
— Mose Durst, *Strategies of Love*

July 20

When faith and hope fail, as they do sometimes, we must try charity, which is love in action. We must speculate no more on our duty, but simply do it.
— Dinah Maria Mulock

God does not ask your ability or your inability. He asks only your availability.
— Mary Kay Ash

July 21

My mother drew a distinction between achievement and success. She said that "achievement is the knowledge that you have studied and worked hard and done the best that is in you. Success is being praised by others, and that's nice, too, but not as important or satisfying. Always aim for achievement and forget about success."
— Helen Hayes

July 22

I could not say I believe. I know! I have had the experience of being gripped by something other than myself, something that people call God.
— Carl G. Jung

I don't care what they say with their mouths — everybody knows that something is eternal. And it ain't houses, and it ain't names, and it ain't earth, and it ain't even stars — everybody knows in their bones that something is eternal, and that something has to do with human beings. All the greatest people ever lived have been telling us that for five thousand years and yet you'd be surprised how people are always losing hold of it. There's something way down deep that's eternal about every human being.
— Thornton Wilder, *Our Town*

July 23

Be of good courage, all is before you, and time passed in the difficult is never lost. . . . What is required of us is that we love the difficult and learn to deal with it. In the difficult are the friendly forces, the hands that work on us.
— Rainer Maria Rilke

July 24

I long to accomplish a great and noble task, but it is my chief duty to accomplish humble tasks as though they were great and noble. The world is moved along by the mighty shoves of its heroes, but also by the aggregate of the tiny pushes of each honest worker.
— Helen Keller

It is the art of mankind to polish the world, and everyone who works is scrubbing in some part.
— Henry David Thoreau

July 25

THE SIN OF OMISSION
Margaret E. Sangster

It isn't the thing you do, dear,
It's the thing you leave undone
That gives you a bit of a heartache
At setting of the sun.
The tender word forgotten,
The letter you did not write,
The flowers you did not send, dear,
Are your haunting ghosts at night.

The stone you might have lifted
Out of a brother's way;
The bit of heartsome counsel
You were hurried too much to say;
The loving touch of the hand, dear,
The gentle, winning tone
Which you had no time nor thought for
With troubles enough of your own.

July 26

It is best to look at problems as gifts to be unwrapped. That is what they are, and they never stop coming. There never comes a time of such mastery that life becomes a vacation resort we can lounge around in. But, from a spiritual perspective, problems become appreciable.
— Polly Berrien Berens

July 27

From a Sermon by an African Preacher

It has been told me once, and twice have I seen this with my own eyes, how the rhinoceros is accompanied by a little bird which ever gives a shrill cry of warning at the imminent approach of danger.

And this is wonderful! Since the rhinoceros is so curiously made in his head that he can only see what is straight in front of him, and so would otherwise be at the mercy of what approaches him from the side. Who else but God could let so small a creature guide so large a one?

My children, have you not noticed how the herds of antelopes graze near one or two giraffes? And have you not asked your hearts why this should be so?

I am the one who can tell you truly. It is because the antelope may have better sight and hearing; but the giraffe, by ever turning his tall and delicate head on his long neck, has the better sight and wider range of view. So that when the wind is away from the antelopes, they watch the behavior of the giraffes, whether they be uneasy or apprehensive of danger. And when the wind is toward them, the giraffes rely on the antelopes. As God's other family, even so do ye, my children.

July 28

Once there was a little bunny who wanted to run away.
So he said to his mother, "I am running away."
"If you run away," said his mother, "I will run after you.
For you are my little bunny."
— Margaret Wise Brown, *The Runaway Bunny*

Nobody has ever measured, even poets, how much a heart can hold.
— Zelda Fitzgerald

July 29

There is one elementary truth, the ignorance of which kills countless ideas and splendid plans. The moment one definitely commits oneself, then providence moves too. All sorts of things occur to help one that would never otherwise have occurred. A whole stream of events issues from the decision, raising in one's favor all manner of unforeseen incidents and meetings and material assistance which no man could have dreamed would have come his way. Whatever you can do or dream you can, begin it. Boldness has genius, power and magic in it. Begin it now.
— Attributed to Goethe

FILLED WITH LIGHT

The one who has seen his foot in an x-ray machine, such as are kept in the shoe-fitting departments of many stores, has seen his foot in a different light. It is not seen as a solid and impenetrable thing covered with skin but as a shape made up of light, the bones being merely a shadow in that light.

"But that is not the reality," we may say.

Why not? We are seeing the foot illuminated by a greater light. Why may not that more intense light-vibration show as a true reality as the naked eye can see?

Science tells us that it does, for the body is not made up of matter but of energy, open and penetrable to the various forces in the air. Sunlight penetrates the open spaces of the body. The vibrations of electric shock treatments can be sent through apparently solid flesh. The light of the x-ray and radium shines through the body as easily as if it were made of light itself, as indeed it is.

And above and beyond all these, a spiritual light vibration penetrates and fills every cell of the body. In other words, we are porous like a sponge and filled with God.

— Agnes Sanford

July 31

Prayer should be the key of the day and the lock of the night.
— Old proverb

Prayer and action are interwoven. If you do not do what you pray about, your prayer life will become shallow. Prayer without action is nothing. You must act upon what you pray; otherwise, nothing will happen.
— Paul Werner

August 1

The horizon leans forward,
Offering you space
To place new steps of change
Here, on the pulse of this fine day
You may have the courage
To look up and out and upon me,
The Rock, the River, the Tree, your country.
No less to Midas than the mendicant.
No less to you now than the mastodon then.

Here on the pulse of this new day
You may have the grace to look up and out
And into your sister's eyes,
And into your brother's face,
Your country,
And say simply
Very simply
With hope—
Good morning.

— Maya Angelou, *On the Pulse of Morning*

August 2

It is not within man's power to place the divine teachings directly in his heart. All that we can do is place them in the surface of the heart so that when the heart breaks they will drop in.
— Hasidic anecdote

AUGUST 3

One who returns to a place sees it with new eyes. Although the place may not have changed, the viewer inevitably has. For the first time things invisible become suddenly visible.
— Louis L'Amour, *Bendigo Shafter*

It takes more than a sudden leap of faith to change a life. It takes a conscious act, a decision to take our life into our hands.
— Mildred Newman and Bernard Berkowitz

August 4

Rabbi Baruqa of Huza often went to the marketplace at Lapet. One day, the prophet Elijah appeared to him there, and Rabbi Baruqa asked him, "Is there anyone among all these people who will have a share in the World to Come?" Elijah answered, "There is none." Later, two men came to the marketplace, and Elijah said to Rabbi Baruqa, "These two will have a share in the World to Come!" Rabbi Baruqa asked the newcomers, "What is your occupation?" They replied, "We are clowns. When we see someone who is sad, we cheer him up. When we see two people quarreling, we try to make peace among them."
— Talmud, Taanit 22a

The Bonus of Laughter
Life pays a bonus to those who learn that laughter is a vital part of living. It is one of God's richest gifts. The Lord loves a cheerful giver, but He also loves the cheerful. And so does everyone else.
— Edwin Davis

August 5

Whatever the world may say or do, my part is to keep myself good; just as a gold piece, or an emerald, or a purple robe insists perpetually, "Whatever the world may say or do, my part is to remain an emerald and keep my color true."
Marcus Aurelius, *Meditations*

August 6

Aim for success, not perfection. Never give up your right to be wrong, because then you will lose the ability to learn new things and move forward with your life. Remember that fear always lurks behind perfectionism. Confronting your fears and allowing yourself the right to be human can, paradoxically, make you a far happier and more productive person.
— Dr. David M. Burns

What would you attempt to do if you knew you could not fail?
— Dr. Robert Schuller

August 7

If I had a formula for bypassing trouble, I would not pass it round. Trouble creates a capacity to handle it. I don't embrace trouble; that's as bad as treating it as an enemy. But I do say meet it as a friend, for you'll see a lot if it and had better be on speaking terms with it.
— Oliver Wendell Holmes

August 8

When I stand before God at the end of my life, I would hope that I would not have a single bit of talent left and could say, "I used everything you gave to me."
— Erma Bombeck

Children, you must remember something. A man without ambition is dead. A man with ambition but no love is dead. A man with ambition and love for his blessings here on earth is ever so alive. Having been alive, it won't be hard in the end to lie down and rest.
— Pearl Bailey, *Talking to Myself*

August 9

A Safe Home

God is the presence, warm, all-enfolding, touching the drab world into brilliance, lifting the sad heart into song, indescribable, beyond understanding, yet by a bird's note, a chord of music, a light at sunset, a sudden movement of rapt insight, a touch of love, making the whole universe a safe home for the soul.
— An early Christian mystic

August 10

African tradition deals with life as an experience to be lived. In many respects, it is much like the Eastern philosophies in that we see ourselves as a part of a life force; we are joined, for instance, to the air, to the earth. We are part of the whole-life process. We live in accordance with, in a kind of correspondence with the rest of the world as a whole. And therefore living becomes an experience, rather than a problem, no matter how bad or how painful it may be.
— Audre Lorde

There is nothing which human courage will not undertake, and little that human patience will not endure.

AUGUST 11

Recently, many of us have begun to ask again about the role of the family and the values embodied in families: discipline, hard work, ambition, self-sacrifice, patience, love. It is easy enough to mock such values as bourgeois. But middle-class or not, they increasingly appear to constitute the spiritual foundation for achievement.
— Clifton Wharton

[The family] is our most important social institution. And it is perfectly clear that its decline has been disastrous for many of our youth. As individuals, most of us believe in the family. We want strong families, we presumably want government policies that help families; we want educational and other cultural institutions to support the family; and we try to foster habits and practices that strengthen the family. Yet, as a society, we are distracted by so many currents and cross-currents that, while we earnestly try to help our young people, we tend to lose sight of this basic fact: without strong families, many of our other efforts will be in vain.
— William J. Bennett,
Our Children & Our Country

August 12

Creative Imagination

It was in West Africa in 1927 that a blood specimen was taken from a black native named Asibi who was sick with yellow fever. This specimen was inoculated into a rhesus monkey which had just been received from India. Asibi recovered but the monkey died of the disease. All the vaccine manufactured since 1927, both by the Rockefeller Foundation and other agencies as well, derives from the original strain of virus obtained from this humble native. Carried down from the present day from one laboratory and by enormous multiplication, it has offered immunity to yellow fever to millions of people in many countries. Through the creative imagination of science, the blood of one man in West Africa has been made to serve the whole human race.
— Rockefeller Foundation Report

What was the least expected is the more highly esteemed.
— Baltaser Gracian, *The Oracle*

August 13

With a good conscience our only sure reward, with history the final judge of our deeds, let us go forth to lead the land we love, asking His blessing and His help, but knowing that here on earth God's work must truly be our own.
— John F. Kennedy

Nothing bigger can come from a human being than to love a great cause more than love itself and to have the privilege of working for it.
— Anna Howard Shaw

August 14

Man's spiritual nature, the vital force which dwells in him, is essentially one and indivisible. That which we call imagination, fancy, understanding, and so forth, are but different figures of the same power of insight, all indissolubly connected with each other; so that if we knew one of them, we might know all of them.

Morality itself, what we call the moral quality of a man, what is this but another side of the one vital force whereby he is and works?

All that a man does is typical of him. You may see how a man would fight by the way in which he sings. His courage, or want of courage, is visible in the word he utters, in the opinion he has formed, no less than in the stroke he strikes.

He is one, and preaches the same self abroad in all these ways.

— Thomas Carlyle

August 15

The whole course of human history may depend on a change of heart in one solitary and even humble individual — for it is in the solitary mind and soul of the individual that the battle between good and evil is waged and ultimately won or lost.
— M. Scott Peck, M.D., *People of the Lie*

August 16

In marriage, I see a principle that seems to me to be vital for a marriage to move into its spiritual reality. I see marriage as a triangle with God at the apex and the husband on one side and the wife on the other side of the base. They are both journeying up the sides concentrating on their own spiritual quest and joying in the companionship of the other as a helpmate. In this, there is a back-and-forth leadership. Say that the wife sees a piece of the truth in a clear, clean way and moves upward on her side of the triangle. . . . If either of them gets their ego involved and refuses to be open to the other, they will stay stuck where they are until the pain gets so intense they will finally be willing to get unstuck.
— Jess Lair, *How to Have a Perfect Marriage*

Love is a choice — not simply, or necessarily, a rational choice, but rather a willingness to be present to others without pretense or guile.
— Carter Heyward, *Our Passion for Justice*

August 17

A man ought to carry himself in the world as an orange tree would if it could walk up and down in the garden, swinging perfume from every little censer it holds up in the air.
— Henry Ward Beecher

The sandlewood tree imparts its fragrance even to the axe that hews it.
— Hindu proverb

August 18

Like all cultures, one of the family's first jobs is to persuade its members they're special, more wonderful than the neighboring barbarians. The persuasion consists of stories showing family members demonstrating admirable traits, which it claims are family traits. Attention to the stories' actual truth is never the family's most compelling consideration. Encouraging belief is. The family's survival depends on the shared sensibility of its members.
— Elizabeth Stone,
Black Sheep and Kissing Cousins

Keep away from people who try to belittle your ambitions. Small people always do that, but the really great make you feel that you, too, can become great.
— Mark Twain

August 19

There is only one prayer—that prayer is, "Teach me how to serve." There is no greater work, no greater love, no greater religion, no greater philosophy than that you say, "I want to serve the Great White Spirit and His children." It matters not which way you serve, whether by bringing the truth of the spiritual part of the Law, or whether you feed those who are hungry or take away all the darkness in men's hearts. It does not matter which way, so long as you serve.

The more you learn how to forget yourself and to serve others, the more you help to develop the spirit . . . within each one of you. It is all very simple.

— Teachings of Silver Birch

August 20

Self-confrontation (is) absolutely essential: we cannot, must not, hide from ourselves; we must face the worst of ourselves (or our shadow) and acknowledge it. The higher morality requires confronting the shadowy one within us who has made the rules necessary in the first place.
— John Sanford, *The Kingdom Within*

What kind of world
would this world be,
If everyone in it
were just like me?

A thought transfixed me: for the first time in my life I saw the truth as it is set into song by so many poets, proclaimed as the final wisdom by so many thinkers. The truth — that love is the ultimate and the highest goal to which man can aspire. Then I grasped the meaning of the greatest secret that human poetry and human thought and belief have to impart: the salvation of man is through love and in love.
— Victor Frankl, *Man's Search for Meaning*

August 22

Long Road To Freedom

Chorus: It's a long road to freedom
A-winding steep and high.
But when you walk in love
With the wind on your wings
And cover the earth
With the songs you sing,
The miles fly by.

I walked one morning by the sea
And all the waves reached out to me
I took their tears and let them be.

I walked one morning at the dawn
While bits of night still lingered on;
I sought my star but it was gone.

I walked one morning with a friend
And prayed the day would never end;
The years have flown, so why pretend.

I walked one morning with my King
And all my winters turned to spring,
Yet every moment held its sting.

August 23

A man with a violin case under his arm stood in Times Square looking lost. He asked a policeman, "How can I get to Carnegie Hall?" The policeman answered, "Practice, man, practice." There is no other short cut to sanctity either.
— Peter Kreeft, *Back to Virtue*

August 24

A missionary was sitting at her second-story window when she was handed a letter from home. As she opened the letter, a crisp, new, ten-dollar bill fell out. She was pleasantly surprised, but as she read the letter her eyes were distracted by the movement of a shabbily dressed stranger down below, leaning against a post in front of the building. She couldn't get him off her mind. Thinking that he might be in greater financial stress than she, she slipped the bill into an envelope on which she quickly penned, "Don't despair." She threw it out the window. The stranger below picked it up, read it, looked up, and smiled as he tipped his hat and went his way.

The next day she was about to leave the house when a knock came at the door. She found the same shabbily dressed man smiling as he handed her a roll of bills.

"That's the sixty bucks you won, lady. Don't Despair paid five to one."

— Charles Swindoll,
Growing Strong in the Seasons of Life

The Twelve Steps

1. We admitted that we were powerless; that our lives had become unmanageable.
2. Came to believe that a power greater than ourselves could restore us to sanity.
3. Made a decision to turn our will and our lives over to the care of God as we understand him.
4. Made a searching and fearless moral inventory of ourselves.
5. Admitted to God, to ourselves, and to another human being the exact nature of our wrongs.
6. Were entirely ready to have God remove all these defects of character.
7. Humbly asked him to remove our shortcomings.
8. Make a list of all persons we had harmed, and become willing to make amends to them all.
9. Make direct amends to such people wherever possible except where to do so would injure them or others.
10. Continued to take personal inventory and when we were wrong promptly admitted it.
11. Sought through prayer and meditation to improve our conscious contact with God as we understand him, praying only for knowledge of his will for us and the power to carry that out.
12. Having had a spiritual awakening as the result of these steps, we tried to carry this message to others and to practice these principles in all our affairs.

August 26

Two prisoners in contingent cells communicate by blows struck on the wall. The wall is what separates them, but also what permits them to communicate. So it is with us and God. Every separation is a bond.
— Simone Weil

Do not let us speak of darker days, let us rather speak of sterner days. These are not dark days: these are great days—the greatest days our country has ever lived; and we must all thank God that we have been allowed, each of us according to our stations, to play a part in making these days memorable in the history of our race.
— Winston Churchill

Upon the fields of friendly strife
Are sown the seeds
That, upon other fields, on other days
Will bear the fruits of victory.
— Douglas MacArthur

August 28

An American tourist in India stood by in awe as he watched Mother Teresa lovingly clean the infected wounds of a horribly disfigured leper. "Sister," he commented, "I wouldn't do that for a million dollars!" Her response? "Neither would I, brother. Neither would I."

August 29

The crisis of our time
As we are beginning
Slowly and painfully to perceive
Is a crisis not of the hands
But of the hearts.
— Archibald MacLeish

August 30

As mothers and fathers, we must teach children not only to think for themselves but also to make decisions for themselves. Otherwise, they will grow up to be adults with little or no capability to make intelligent decisions for their own lives, much less for their society and their planet. And whether we like it or not, we are living at a momentous time on earth when our capacity to find the best within ourselves and live from that place and change the world accordingly may possibly determine whether or not we survive.

What could be more important for the future of our world than that we raise happy and well-adjusted, empowered and empowering children? They are the caretakers of tomorrow's world, and they will be ready for the job or not. This is not just a woman's issue; it is the issue most central to our society's healing and growth. Every woman and every man, too, must take responsibility in their hearts for all children. As the parental generation, every child is our child. To ignore the state of our children is to ignore the state of our world.

— Marianne Williamson, *A Woman's Worth*

August 31

Be content with what you have; rejoice in the way things are. When you realize there is nothing lacking, the whole world belongs to you.
— Lao Tzu

Normal day, let me be aware of the treasure you are. Let me learn from you, love you, bless you before you depart. Let me not pass you by in quest of some rare and perfect tomorrow. Let me hold you while I may, for it may not always be so. One day I shall dig my nails into the earth, or bury my face in the pillow, or stretch myself taut, or raise my hands to the sky and want, more than all the world, your return.
— Mary Jean Irion, *Yes, World*

SEPTEMBER 1

It is not easy to fall out of the hands of the living God for they are so large and they cradle so much of a man. It is a long time before a man can get himself away; even through the greatest blasphemies the hand of the living God still continues to cradle him.
— D. H. Lawrence

September 2

Once upon a time there was an old woman. Blind. Wise.

One day the woman is visited by some young people who seem to be bent on disproving her clairvoyance and showing her up for the fraud they believe she is. They stand before her, and one of them says,

"Old woman, I hold in my hand a bird. Tell me whether it is living or dead."

She does not answer, and the question is repeated. "Is the bird I am holding living or dead?"

Still she does not answer. She is blind and cannot see her visitors, let alone what is in their hands. She does not know their color, gender or homeland. She only knows their motive.

The old woman's silence is so long, the young people have trouble holding their laughter.

Finally she speaks, and her voice is soft but stern. "I don't know," she says. "I don't know whether the bird you are holding is dead or alive, but what I do know is that it is in your hands. It is in your hands."

Her answer can be taken to mean: if it is dead, you have either found it that way or you have killed it. Whether it is to stay alive is your decision.

— retold by Toni Morrison

September 3

There are many kinds of success in life worth having. It is exceedingly interesting and attractive to be a successful businessman, a railroad man, farmer, or a successful lawyer or doctor; or a writer, or a president, or a ranchman, or the colonel of a fighting regiment or to kill grizzly bears and lion. But for unflagging interest and enjoyment, a household of children, if things go reasonably well, certainly makes all other forms of success and achievement lose their importance by comparison.
— Theodore Roosevelt

September 4

Men do not care how nobly they live, but only how long, although it is within the reach of every man to live nobly, but within no man's power to live long.
— Seneca

What lies before us and what lies behind us is but a small matter compared to what lies within us.
— Ralph Waldo Emerson

September 5

Faith is not making religious-sounding noises in the daytime. It is asking your inmost self questions at night — and then getting up and going to work.
— Mary Jean Irion, *Yes, World*

Inherently, each one of us has the substance within to achieve whatever our goals and dreams define. What is missing from each of us is the training, education, knowledge and insight to utilize what we already have.
— Mark Twain

September 6

If it can be verified, we don't need faith.... Faith is for that which lies on the other side of reason. Faith is what makes life bearable, with all its tragedies and ambiguities and sudden, startling joys.
— Madeleine L'Engle,
Walking on Water: Reflections on Faith and Art

Make a prayer acknowledging yourself as a vehicle of light, giving thanks for the good that has come that day and an affirmation of intent to live in harmony with all your relations.
— Dhyani Ywahoo

September 7

He was really very sorry for what he had done. So he crept downstairs and opened the front door quite softly, and went out into the garden. But when the children saw him they were so frightened that they all ran away, and the garden became winter again. Only the little boy did not run, for his eyes were so full of tears that he did not see the Giant coming. And the Giant stole up behind him and took him gently in his hand, and put him in the tree. And the tree broke at once into blossom, and the birds came and sang on it, and the little boy stretched out his two arms and flung them around the Giant's neck and kissed him. And the other children when they saw that the Giant was not wicked any longer, came running back, and with them came the Spring. "It is your garden now, little children," said the Giant, and he took a great axe and knocked down the wall. And when the poeple were going to market at twelve o'clock, they found the Giant playing with the children in the most beautiful garden they had ever seen.

— Oscar Wilde, *The Selfish Giant*

September 8

Humanity is like a bird with its two wings — the one is male, the other female. Unless both wings are strong and impelled by some common force, the bird cannot fly heavenwards. According to the spirit of this age, women must advance and fulfill their mission in all departments of life . . . . This is my earnest prayer and it is one of the fundamental principles of Bahá'u'lláh.
— 'Abdu'l-Bahá

Man is born for the sake of woman, and woman is born for the sake of man. If you assert your ego, God leaves your marriage; if you respect your spouse, God will come in. A couple should walk together as two legs in harmony, balancing each other, not as one unsteady leg.

September 9

Character is something each one of us must build for himself, out of the laws of God and nature, the examples of others, and — most of all — out of the trials and errors of daily life. Character is the total of thousands of small daily strivings to live up to the best that is in us. Character is the final decision to reject whatever is demeaning to oneself or to others and with confidence and honesty to choose the right.
— Arthur G. Trudeau

September 10

All the powerful things in the world are invisible — honor, character, love, your power to visualize and make dreams come true. They are lights within, casting their rays around you so that you can find your way. Open your eyes with faith so that you can see them.
— Celia Caroline Cole

SEPTEMBER 11

Never doubt that a small group of thoughtful, committed citizens can change the world. Indeed, it is the only thing that ever has.
— Margaret Mead

Do not wait for leaders; do it alone, person to person.
— Mother Teresa

September 12

It is only by going down into the abyss that we recover the treasures of life. Where you stumble, there lies your treasure. The very cave you are afraid to enter turns out to be the source of what you were looking for.
— Joseph Campbell

SEPTEMBER 13

I have learned this at least by my experiment: that if one advances confidently in the direction of his dreams, and endeavors to live the life he has imagined, he will meet with a success unexpected in common hours.
— Henry David Thoreau

September 14

To nurture a child's spirit is not to provide him or her with lessons on religion or morality. We don't do spiritual nurture by setting up a schedule of specific "activities." In all the great religious traditions, spiritual growth is understood as a journey. It is a path or a way along which each human being travels, not only in moments of ecstasy or enlightenment, but in the day-to-day struggle to come to terms with the world in which we live. For this reason, spiritual nurture, like parenting itself, is a creative process. It is a work of the imagination. We need not worry about having all the answers. We need only be willing to accompany our child as she takes her first steps along the spiritual path. We see her with God's eyes, to "embrace" her, in Martin Buber's word, as a unique creation whose worth is infinitely greater than the sum of her skills and knowledge. And we come to know ourselves as spiritual beings, to be willing to bring our own hearts to rest on that which is truly central.
— Jean Grasso Fitzpatrick, *Something More*

September 15

What is hateful to yourself, do not to your fellow man. That is the whole of the Torah and the remainder is but commentary. Go, learn it.

The mitzvah, the humble single act of serving God, of helping man, of cleansing the self, is our way of dealing with the problem [of evil].
There is always an opportunity to do a mitzvah, and precious is life because at all times and in all places we are able to do His will. This is why despair is alien to Jewish faith.

September 16

This is the true joy in life, being used for a purpose recognized by yourself as a mighty one.
Being a force of nature instead of a feverish, selfish little clod of ailments and grievances complaining that the world will not devote itself to making you happy.
I am of the opinion that my life belongs to the whole community and as I live it is my privilege — my privilege to do for it whatever I can.
I want to be thoroughly used up when I die, for the harder I work the more I love. I rejoice in life for its own sake. Life is no brief candle to me; it is a sort of splendid torch which I've got a hold of for the moment and I want to make it burn as brightly as possible before handing it on to future generations.
— George Bernard Shaw, in Stephen R. Covey, *Principle-Centered Leadership*

September 17

For every thing there is a season, and a time for every purpose under the heaven: A time to be born, and a time to die; a time to plant, and a time to pluck up that which is planted; A time to kill and a time to heal; a time to break down, and a time to build up; A time to weep, and a time to laugh; a time to mourn, and a time to dance; A time to cast away stones, and a time to gather stones together; a time to embrace, and a time to refrain from embracing; A time to get, and a time to lose; a time to keep, and a time to cast away; A time to rend, and a time to sew; a time to keep silence, and a time to speak; A time to love, and a time to hate; a time of war, and a time of peace.
— Ecclesiastes

September 18

Morning is the time to recapture the momentum which will stay with us throughout the day. Go over your goals and plans with God; then at the end of the day, share your victories and repent for your shortcomings.
— Nora Spurgin

A person, if he is to be spiritually healthy, ought to worship more than once a week and in more than one sanctuary. There should be more than one place in everybody's life where he is refreshed, restored, and rebuilt. A soul can no more maintain robust spiritual health on one worship experience per week than he can live on one meal each week. The soul of man must eat regularly or sicken and die.
— Harold E. Kohn

September 19

There are so many disciplines in being a parent besides the obvious ones like getting up in the night and putting up with the noise during the day. And almost the hardest of all is learning to be a well of affection and not a fountain, to show them we love them, not when we feel like it, but when they do.
— Nan Fairbrother, *An English Year*

September 20

1. We are interdependent.
2. We take individual responsibility for all we do.
3. We must treat others as we wish others to treat us.
4. We consider humankind our family.
5. We must strive for a just social and economic order, in which everyone has an equal chance of reaching his or her full potential.
6. We commit ourselves to a culture of respect, justice and peace.
7. Earth cannot be changed for the better unless the consciousness or individuals is changed first.

— From the Parliament of the World's Religions

September 21

A person can run for years but sooner or later he has to take a stand in the place which, for better or worse, he calls home, and do what he can to change things there.
— Paule Marshall,
The Chosen Place, the Timeless People

It is better to do a good deed
near home than to travel
a thousand miles to burn incense.
— Chinese Proverb

September 22

Once upon a time a king gathered some blind men about an elephant and asked them to tell him what an elephant was like. The first man felt a tusk and said an elephant was like a giant carrot; another happened to touch an ear and said it was like a big fan; another touched its trunk and said it was like a pestle; still another, who happened to feel its leg, said it was like a mortar; and another, who grasped its tail said it was like a rope. Not one of them was able to tell the king the elephant's real form. In like manner, one might partly describe the true nature of a human being.
—The Teaching of Buddha

September 23

Any lover knows that to end a quarrel the simple gesture of bringing a red rose goes a long way. Acts that would produce a constructive emotional impact on one side often involve little or no cost to the other. A note of sympathy, a statement of regret, a visit to the cemetery, delivering a small present for a grandchild, shaking hands or embracing, eating together — all may be priceless opportunities to improve a hostile emotional situation at small cost. On many occasions an apology can defuse emotions effectively.... An apology may be one of the least costly and most rewarding investments you can make.
— Roger Fisher and William Ury, *Getting to Yes*

When a friend is in trouble, don't annoy him by asking if there is anything you can do. Think up something appropriate and do it.
— E. W. Howe

September 24

Indeed, the truth that many people never understand, until it is too late, is that the more you try to avoid suffering, the more you suffer, because smaller and more significant things begin to torture you, in proportion to your fear of being hurt. The one who does most to avoid suffering is, in the end, the one who suffers most: and his suffering comes to him from the things so little and so trivial that one can say that it is no longer objective at all. It is his own existence, his own being, that is at once the subject and the source of his pain, and his very existence and consciousness is his greatest torture.

— Thomas Merton, *The Seven Storey Mountain*

SEPTEMBER 25

I AM YOUR HOME
Percy R. Hayward

I am your home.
I am a bundle of bricks or stone and some wood, I can be sold or brought in the market for a few thousand dollars in money.
But I am more than these. I am —
Thousands of years of human history with the long struggle of mankind for love and protection;
Dreams and visions and aspirations;
Tears and struggles and disappointments that rend the soul apart;
A lull and breathing space in the hot hard struggle of life;
Horny hands and self-discipline and laughter.
They say that I am held together by nails and cement and mortar.
But I am held together by —
Forgiveness that even forgets;
Love that fails not.

Kindness in words creates confidence. Kindness in thinking creates profoundness. Kindness in giving creates love.
— Lao-tzu

Kind words are the music of the world. They have a power which seems to be beyond natural causes, as they were some angel's song which had lost its way and come to earth.
— Frederick William Faber

September 27

Risen Soul

Do not wait for my soul to rise
for it has risen;
You may think I am dead and no
longer with you, but you are wrong.
I will now live for eternity, no drugs;
violence, or killing. It is very peaceful.
I fly freely and watch from above.
Once in a while I come down and
cry with you for I am sad too.
I will miss the laughing, the
crying and everything else.
But a new life is now beginning.
This time I will not die.
I will bring joy and happiness
up here as I did down there.
Do not wait for my soul to rise
for it has risen.
— Jessica Powell (Jessica, age 13, wrote this poem for her friend, Lisa Doell, who was killed in a car accident.)

The dead don't die. They look on and help.
— D. H. Lawrence

September 28

He was a mind in a body without a soul. It was a story in a Yiddish book about a poor Jew and his struggles to get to Eretz Yisroel before he died. Ah, how that man suffered! And my Daniel enjoyed the story, he enjoyed the last terrible page, because when he finished it he realized for the first time what a memory he had.

He looked at me proudly and told me back the story from memory and I cried inside my heart.

I went away and cried to the Master of the Universe, "What have you done to me? A *mind* like this I need for a son? A *heart* I need for a son, *compassion* I want from my son, righteousness, mercy, strength to suffer and carry pain, that I want from my son, not a mind without a soul!"

— Chaim Potok, *The Chosen*

September 29

We are not unlike a particularly hardy crustacean. . . . With each passage from one stage of human growth to the next we, too, must shed a protective structure. We are left exposed and vulnerable — but also yeasty and embryonic again, capable of stretching in ways we hadn't known before. These sheddings may take several years or more. Coming out of each passage, though, we enter a longer and more stable period in which we can expect relative tranquility and a sense of equilibrium regained.
— Gail Sheehy, *Passages*

Our consciousness rarely registers the beginning of a growth within us any more than without us: there have been many circulations of the sap before we detect the smallest sign of the bud.
— George Eliot, *Silas Marner*

Prayer is not easy. It is not the speaking of many words, or the hypnotic spell of the recited formula; it is the raising of the heart and mind to God in constantly renewed acts of love. We must go forward to grapple with prayer, as Jacob wrestled with the angel. We must lift high our lamp of Faith that it may show us what prayer is, and what are its power and dignity. Into the darkness we must whisper our prayer: Lord, teach us how to pray . . . it is a concept which will take us our whole life to fathom, and a practice which our whole life will be too short to perfect.

— Karl Rahner on Prayer

October 1

Take a chance! All life is a chance. The man who goes the furthest is generally the one who is willing to do and dare.
— Dale Carnegie

Don't be afraid to take a big step if one is indicated. You can't cross a chasm in two small jumps.
— David Lloyd George

October 2

Be brave enough to live life creatively. The creative is the place where no one else has ever been. You have to leave the city of your comfort and go into the wilderness of your intuition. You can't get there by bus, only by hard work and risk and by not quite knowing what you're doing. What you'll discover will be wonderful. What you'll discover will be yourself.
— Alan Alda

October 3

You gain strength, courage and confidence by every experience in which you really stop to look fear in the face. You are able to say to yourself, "I have lived through this horror. I can take the next thing that comes along." You must do the thing you think you cannot do.
— Eleanor Roosevelt

The way you overcome shyness is to become so wrapped up in something that you forget to be afraid.
— Lady Bird Johnson

Make chastity your furnace, patience your smithy, The Master's word your anvil, and true knowledge your hammer.
Make awe of God your bellows, and with it kindle the fire of austerity.
And in the crucible of love, melt the nectar Divine.
Only in such a mint, can men be cast into the World.
— Adi Granth, Japuji 38, M,1

October 5

It is because of grace that it is possible for people to transcend the traumas of loveless parenting and become themselves loving individuals who have risen far above their parents on the scale of human evolution. Why, then, do only some people spiritually grow and evolve beyond the circumstances of their parentage? I believe that grace is available to everyone, that we are all cloaked in the love of God, no one less nobly than another. The only answer I can give, therefore, is that most of us choose not to heed the call of grace and to reject its assistance. Christ's assertion, "Many are called, but few are chosen," I would translate to mean "All of us are called by and to grace, but few of us choose to listen to the call."
— M. Scott Peck, M.D., *The Road Less Travelled*

Men stumble over the truth from time to time, but most pick themselves up and hurry off as if nothing happened.
— Winston Churchill

October 6

Though he be ever so tired by repeated failure, let him begin his operations again and again; for fortune greatly favors the man who perseveres in his undertakings.
— Laws of Manu 9.300

There is no failure except in no longer trying.
— Elbert Hubbard

October 7

You have to stick to your plan. A lot of people try to pull you down to their level because they can't achieve certain things. But very few people get anywhere by taking shortcuts. Very few people win the lottery to gain their wealth. It happens, but the odds certainly aren't with them. More people get it the honest way, by setting their goals and committing themselves to achieving those goals.

— Michael Jordan, *I Can't Accept Not Trying*

October 8

Live with men as if God saw you, and talk to God as if men were listening.
— Athenodorus

General Colin L. Powell remembers a lesson learned while mopping floors at a local soft-drink bottling plant:
Someone once told me a story about three ditch diggers. One leaned on his shovel and talked about owning the company. Another complained about the hours and the pay. The third just kept digging. Years went by, and the first guy was still leaning on that shovel. The second guy had retired on disability after a phony injury. And the third guy? He owned the company.
The moral is, no matter what you do, someone is always watching. So I set out to be the best mop wielder there ever was. One day someone let 50 cases of cola crash to the concrete, and brown sticky foam cascaded across the floor. It was almost more than I could bear. But I kept mopping, right to left, left to right. At summer's end, the foreman had me filling bottles. The third summer, I was deputy foreman. As I have learned, someone is always watching.
— *Guideposts*

October 9

The mandate to "love your neighbor as you love yourself" is not just a moral mandate. It's a psychological mandate. Caring is biological. One thing you can get from caring for others is you're not lonely. And the more connected you are to life the healthier you are.
— James Lynch

Be kind — remember every one you meet is fighting a battle — everybody's lonesome.
— Marion Parker

OCTOBER 10

TO MOVE THE MASSES
Elizabeth Barrett Browning

It takes a soul
To move a body; it takes a high-minded man
To move the masses, even to a cleaner style;
It takes the ideal, to blow a hair's breadth off
The dust of the actual — Ah, your couriers failed
Because not poet enough to understand
That life develops from within.

Joy is in character, not in condition; its sources are within rather than without.
— Joong Hyun Pak

October 11

I'm living in a house and I know I built it. I work in a workshop which was constructed by me. I speak a language which I developed. And I know I shape my life according to my desires by my own ability. I feel I am safe. I can defend myself. I am not afraid. This is the greatest happiness a man can feel — that he could be a partner with the Lord in creation. This is the real happiness of man — creative life, conquest of nature, and a great purpose.
— David Ben-Gurion

October 12

Love does not consist in gazing at each other but in looking outward together in the same direction.
— Antoine de St.-Exupery

In that quietness they were speaking their own language, with their eyes, with the way they stood, with what they put into the air about them, each knowing what the other was saying, and having strength from the other, for they had been learning through forty years of being together, and their minds were one.
— Richard Llewellyn

October 13

Yes, you have to be willing to take a risk. A man told me that he was thinking of writing a book about Second Lives, about what people have done because of cancer, heart disease, or violence that has struck them. But I don't want people to need a second life, I want you to live this one now.

Life is an opportunity for you to contribute love in your own way. I'd like you to find the strength that I know is there inside you to draw on. Then use that strength and energy and live fully. You will realize that you are a sphere whose center is everywhere and whose circumference is nowhere. Just as one thought affects your entire body, so do you affect everyone else when you change. So give birth to yourself and begin your life. Let the river of your life flow freely and deeply, and let the pebbles of your love fall into the water to create ripples that will touch us all.

— Bernie Siegel, M.D.,
How To Live Between Office Visits

October 14

Oh! I have slipped the surly bonds of Earth
And danced the skies on laughter-slivered wings;
Sunward I've climbed, and joined the tumbling mirth
of sun-split clouds, — and done a hundred things
You have not dreamed of — wheeled and soared and swung
High in the sunlit silence. Hov'ring there,
I've chased the shouting wind along, and flung
My eager craft through footless halls of air
. . .

Up, up the long, delirious, burning blue
I've topped the wind-swept heights with easy grace
Where never lark nor ever eagle flew —
And, while with silent lifting mind I've trod
The high untrespassed sanctity of space,
Put out my hand, and touched the face of God.
— John G. Magee

October 15

The human contribution is the essential ingredient. It is only in the giving of oneself to others that we truly live.
— Ethel Percy Andrus

Life begets life. Energy creates energy. It is by spending oneself that one becomes rich.
— Sarah Bernhardt

October 16

The five most important words:
I am proud of you.
The four most important words:
What is your opinion?
The three most important words:
If you please.
The two most important words:
Thank you.
The least important word:
"I."

OCTOBER 17

P'I Standstill (Stagnation)
In times of stagnation, attend to your attitude.
— I Ching

Life is what we make it, always has been, always will be.
— Grandma Moses

OCTOBER 18

Marriage, which is the will of two to create something beyond themselves, is a participation in God's creative power. In our spiritual life this participation should awaken all our energies for God's essence, His will, and His love to all. [As baptism] . . . is absolutely unrepeatable . . . the same is true of marriage to the one person who is given to each of us for the fulfillment of all his [the spouse] and all our potentialities in life.
— Eberhard Arnold,
Love and Marriage in the Spirit

October 19

One ought, every day at least, to hear a little song, read a good poem, see a fine picture, and if it were possible, to speak a few reasonable words.
— Goethe

When I have nothing to do for an hour, and I don't want to do anything, I neither read nor watch television. I sit back in a chair and let my mind relax. I do what I call idling. It's as if the motorcar's running but you haven't got it in gear. You have to allow a certain amount of time in which you are doing nothing in order to have things occur to you, to let your mind think.
— Mortimer Adler

October 20

Be Thou my vision, O Lord of my heart;
Naught be all else to me, save that Thou art —
Thou my best thought, by day or by night,
Waking or sleeping, Thy presence my light.

Riches I heed not, nor man's empty praise,
Thou mine inheritance, now and always;
Thou and Thou only, first in my heart,
High king of heaven, my treasure Thou art.

October 21

The cures for all the ills and wrongs, the cares, the sorrows, and the crimes of humanity, all lie in the one word "love." It is the divine vitality that everywhere produces and restores life. To each and every one of us, it gives the power of working miracles.
— Lydia M. Child

Where there is great love there are always miracles.
— Willa Cather

October 22

To take the difficulties, setbacks and sorrows of life as a challenge which to overcome makes us stronger, rather than as unjust punishment which should not happen to us, requires faith and courage.
— Erich Fromm, *The Art of Loving*

A problem is a chance for you to do your best.
— Duke Ellington

October 23

Then how can you attract others' love? By giving love. In other words, your love passes through the other person and then returns to you. God created man to be this way. Man cannot live alone, he must live together with others. If I give love to others they will return love to me. If I just seek love, however, there won't be any connection. If we always wait for others to initiate, nothing will ever happen. Everyone just waits and sees, waiting and waiting for love to come. How can it possibly come? If we try to give love it comes back immediately. This is give and take. For this reason we must give love first. If we only want to receive love there will be no action or motion, everything will be frozen.

Give first, then you can receive. This is a very simple thing, but we don't understand it so well. Giving is not giving away, giving is having.
— Young Whi Kim
Guidance for Heavenly Tradition

When I left home and faced the realities of the world, I put my thoughts of God in cold storage for a while, because I couldn't reconcile what I believed, deep inside, with what was going on around me. But that early period, when God was as real as the wind which blew from the sea through the pine trees in the garden, left me with inner peace, which, as I grew older, swelled — until, perforce, I had to open my mind to God again.
— Jane Goodall

In the darkest hour the soul is replenished and given strength to continue and endure.
— Heart Warrior Chosa

October 25

"What is REAL?" asked the Rabbit one day, when they were lying side by side near the nursery fender, before Nana came to tidy the room. "Does it mean having things that buzz inside you and a stick-out handle?"

"Real isn't how you are made," said the Skin Horse. "It's a thing that happens to you. When a child loves you for a long, long time, not just to play with, but REALLY loves you, then you become Real."

"Does it hurt?" asked the Rabbit.

"Sometimes," said the Skin Horse, for he was always truthful. "When you are Real you don't mind being hurt."

"Does it happen all at once, like being wound up," he asked, "or bit by bit?"

"It doesn't happen all at once," said the Skin Horse. "You become. It takes a long time. That's why it doesn't often happen to people who break easily, or have sharp edges, or have to be carefully kept. Generally, by the time you are Real, most of your hair has been loved off, and your eyes drop out and you get loose in the joints and very shabby. But these things don't matter at all, because once you are real you can't be ugly, except to people who don't understand."

— Margery Williams, *The Velveteen Rabbit*

October 26

There are many ways of breaking a heart. Stories were full of hearts broken by love, but what really broke a heart was taking away its dream — whatever that dream might be.
— Pearl S. Buck

Don't be afraid of the space between your dreams and reality. If you can dream it, you can make it so.
— Belva Davis

October 27

Perhaps you have heard the story of Christopher Wren, one of the greatest of English architects, who walked one day unrecognized among the men who were at work upon the building of St. Paul's Cathedral in London which he had designed. "What are you doing?" he inquired of one of the workmen, and the man replied, "I am cutting a piece of stone." As he went on he put the same question to another man, and the man replied, "I am earning five shillings twopence a day." And to a third man he addressed the same inquiry and the man answered, "I am helping Sir Christopher Wren build a beautiful cathedral." That man had vision. He could see beyond the cutting of the stone, beyond the earning of his daily wage, to the creation of a work of art — the building of a great cathedral. And in your life it is important for you to strive to attain a vision of the larger whole.
— Louise Bush-Brown

October 28

Lü / Treading (Conduct)
Lasting progress is won
through quiet self-discipline.
— I Ching

To enjoy good health, to bring true happiness to one's family, to bring peace at all, one must first discipline and control one's own mind. If a man can control his mind he can find the way to enlightenment, and all wisdom and virtue will naturally come to him.
Just as treasures are uncovered from the earth, so virtue appears from good deeds, and wisdom appears from a pure and peaceful mind. To walk safely through the maze of human life, one needs the light of wisdom and the guidance of virtue.
— The Teaching of Buddha

OCTOBER 29

Somebody said that it couldn't be done,
But he with a chuckle replied
That "maybe it couldn't," but he would be one
Who wouldn't say so till he tried.
So he buckled right in with the trace of a grin
On his face. If he worried he hid it.
He started to sing as he tackled the thing
That couldn't be done, and he did it.
— Edgar A. Guest

We rejoice in our sufferings, knowing that suffering produces endurance, and endurance produces character, and character produces hope, and hope does not disappoint us, because God's love has been poured into our hearts.
— Romans 5: 3–5

October 31

I don't think of all the misery, but of the beauty that still remains. . . . My advice is: Go outside, to the fields, enjoy nature and the sunshine, go out and try to recapture happiness in yourself and in God. Think of all the beauty that's still left in and around you and be happy!
— Anne Frank

Remember this . . . our world is one where the impossible occurs every day, and what we often call supernatural is simply the misunderstood.
— Louis L'Amour, *The Lonesome Gods*

November 1

You need to get up in the morning and say, "Boy, I'm going to — in my own stupid way — save the world today."
— Carol Bellamy

There are people who put their dreams in a little box and say, "Yes, I've got dreams, of course, I've got dreams." Then they put the box away and bring it out once in a while to look in it, and yep, they're still there. These are great dreams, but they never even get out of the box. It takes an uncommon amount of guts to put your dreams on the line, to hold them up and say, "How good or bad am I?" That's where courage comes in.
— Erma Bombeck

November 2

That a secret plan
Is hid in my hand;
That my hand is big,
Big,
Because of this plan.
That God,
Who dwells in my hand,
Knows this secret plan
Of the things He will do for the world
Using my hand!
—Toyohiko Kagawa

November 3

I share Einstein's affirmation that anyone who is not lost in the rapturous awe at the power and glory of the mind behind the universe "is as good as a burnt out candle."
— Madeleine L'Engle

To me it seems that when God
conceived the world,
that was poetry;
He formed it,
and that was sculpture;
He varied and colored it,
and that was painting;
and then, crowning all,
He peopled it with living things,
and that was the grand, divine,
eternal drama.
— Charlotte Cushman

November 4

I have been driven many times upon my knees by the overwhelming conviction that I had nowhere else to go. My own wisdom, and that of all about me, seemed insufficient for that day.
— Abraham Lincoln

I slept and dreamed that life was happiness.
I awoke and saw that life was service.
I served and found that in service happiness is found.
— Rabindranath Tagore

The fragrance always remains in the hand that gives the rose.
— Heda Bejar, *Peacemaking, Day by Day*

November 6

Hold fast, all together, to God's rope, and be not divided among yourselves. Remember with gratitude God's favor on you, for you were enemies and He joined your hearts in love, so that by His grace you became brethren. You were on the brink of the fiery Pit, and He saved you from it. Thus does God make His signs clear to you, that you may be guided.
Let there arise out of you one community, inviting to all that is good, enjoining what is right, and forbidding what is wrong: those will be prosperous. Be not like those who are divided among themselves and fall into disputations after receiving clear signs: unto them is a dreadful pity.
— Qur'an 3.103–5

A Cup of Warm Milk
Susan Cleghorn

The world itself is a child,
Appalled, bewildered,
Exhausted, supperless,
Roared at and threatened
By drunken old war.
The world needs a cup of milk,
Warm with kindness,
In a fireside corner,
On a low footstool;
A reassuring arm
And a homelike voice.
Quiet; comfort; mothering.

November 8

On your way to heaven, you must expect to experience not only the heavenly side, but also taste the dungeons of hell; in the end, what you go through in hell will become the most precious part of God's grace. In this way you will become strong, and in your process of maturing, you will acquire a wholesome personality that reflects God's own personality. Then you will better appreciate heaven. Someday you will have a record you can be proud of — the chronicle of your victory and perseverance. It will be your source of greatest pride.
— Hak Ja Han Moon

November 9

The first sacrifice of this sort leads the way to others, and a single hand's turn given heartily to the world's great work helps one amazingly with one's own small tasks.
— Louisa May Alcott, *An Old-fashioned Girl*

We must not, in trying to think about how we can make a big difference, ignore the small daily differences we can make which, over time, add up to big differences that we often cannot foresee.
— Marian Wright Edelman, *Families in Peril*

Picture of Life

One bright summer afternoon an artist was standing atop a rocky mountain cliff, painting the beautiful panorama. With every stroke of the brush, he paused to regard his painting from various angles and smile to himself. When he placed the last stroke upon his masterpiece, the artist began stepping backwards in order to obtain a better view of the completed painting. Little did he realize that each step was bringing him nearer to the edge of the cliff. His friend, standing nearby, noticed the artist's danger. Knowing that a warning would be too late, he dashed over to the easel, seized a brush, and smeared the face of the painting. The artist, furious at his friend's behavior, rushed forward to his work and so was saved from destruction.

When the friend explained the precarious position from which he had saved him, the artist was overwhelmed with gratitude and appreciation.

Moral: We find similar instances in life. One who has been living in luxury and comfort forgets the rest of the world and his fellow man. Suddenly an invisible hand reaches out and splashes across his canvas of joy, leaving him destitute and forlorn. He is then compelled to return to that which he had previously forsaken — his people and his religion.

November 11

The idea of coming together — we're still not good at that in this country.

We talk a lot about it. Some politicians call it "family."

In moments of crisis we're magnificent at it — the Depression, Franklin Roosevelt lifting himself from his wheelchair to lift this nation from its knees.

At those moments we understand community — helping one another. In baseball, you do that all the time. You can't win it alone. You can be the best pitcher in baseball but somebody has to get you a run to win the game. It is a community activity. You need all nine people helping one another. I love bunt plays. I love the idea of the bunt. I love the idea of the sacrifice. Even the word is good. Giving yourself up for the good of the whole. That's Jeremiah. That's thousands of years of wisdom. You find your own good in the good of the whole. You find your own individual fulfillment in the success of the communtiy — the Bible tried to teach you that and didn't teach you. Baseball did.

— from an interview with Mario Cuomo

NOVEMBER 12

Father, O mighty Force,
That Force which is in everything,
Come down between us, fill us,
Until we become like thee,
Until we become like thee.
— Susu Prayer (Guinea)

What is man?
Man is not matter; he is not made up of brain, blood, bones and other material elements. The scriptures inform us that man is made in the image and likeness of God. Matter is not that likeness. The likeness of Spirit cannot be so unlike Spirit. Man is spiritual and perfect, he must be so understood in Christian Science. Man is ideal, the image, of Love; he is not physique.
—Mary Baker Eddy, *Science and Health*, 475

November 13

No matter how big and tough a problem may be, get rid of confusion by taking one little step toward solution. Do something. Then try again. At the worst, so long as you don't do it the same way twice, you will eventually use up all the wrong ways of doing it and thus the next try will be the right one.
— G. E. Nordenholt

November 14

Though it may be unessential to the imagination, travel is necessary to an understanding of men. Only with long experience and the opening of his wares on many a beach where his language is not spoken, will the merchant come to know the worth of what he carries, and what is parochial and what is universal in his choice.

Such delicate goods as justice, love and honor, courtesy, and indeed all the things we care for, are valid everywhere; but they are variously molded and often differently handled, and sometimes nearly unrecognizable if you meet them in a foreign land; and the art of learning fundamental common values is perhaps the greatest gain of travel to those who wish to live at ease among their fellows.
— Freya Stark

What is traveling? Changing your place? By no means! Traveling is changing your opinions and prejudices.
— Anatole France

November 15

Wonder and despair are two sides of a spinning coin. When you open yourself to one, you open yourself to the other. You discover a capacity for joy that wasn't in you before. Wonder is the promise of restoration: as deeply as you dive, so you may rise.
— Christina Baldwin, *Life's Companion, Journal Writing as a Spiritual Quest*

November 16

Like one who leaves the trampled street
For some cathedral, cool and dim,
Where he can hear in music beat
The heart of prayer, that beats for him;

And sees the common light of day,
Through painted panes, transfigured, shine,
And casts his human woes away,
In presence of the Woe Divine:

So I, from life's tormenting themes
Turn where the silent chapel lies,
Whose windows burn with vanished dreams,
Whose altar-lights are memories.

There, watched by pitying cherubim,
In sacred hush, I rest awhile,
Till solemn sounds of harp and hymn
Begin to sweep the haunted aisle:

Restored and comforted, I go
To grapple with my tasks again;
Through silent worship taught to know
The blessed peace that follows pain.
— Bayard Taylor, 1825–1878

November 17

The true motivation for prayer is . . . the sense of not being at home in the universe. Is there a sensitive heart that could stand indifferent and feel at home in the sight of so much evil and suffering, in the face of countless failures to live up to the will of God? . . . . The experience of prayer gains intensity in the amazing awareness that God Himself is not at home in the universe.

To pray means to bring God back into the world, to establish His Kingship for a second at least. To pray means to expand His presence.

— Abraham Joshua Heschel

November 18

Man and Woman
equally as can be
Creation, other things
and don't forget Me!
True love, care,
laughter and fun
All working together to
Unite as one
— Kevin Brabazon, age 12

November 19

Once, an old Zen Master sat pouring a cup to overflowing as he faced a college professor seeking enlightenment. "Stop!" said the professor. "Can't you see it's too full?" "And so it is with you," said the old Master. "It is only as you empty that something new can come in."

November 20

Prayer is more than meditation. In meditation the source of strength is one's self. When one prays he goes to a source of strength greater than his own.
— Madame Chiang Kai-shek, *I Confess My Faith*

He prayed as he breathed, forming no words and making no specific requests, only holding in his heart, like broken birds in cupped hands, all those people who were in stress or grief.
— Ellis Peters

THE MICE WHO TALKED
Sheila Vaughn

The mice all held a meeting
to decide what to do with the cat
who ruined most of their parties
and was always on the attack
One mouse said "I've got it!
On his neck we'll hang a bell
so whenever he comes near us
we'll be able to hear him well"

The plan was truly brilliant
A great idea, you bet
But no one would slip the bell
around that old cat's neck
While they were talking,
talking, talking
That cat was stalking,
stalking, stalking
You know it's really not a mystery
Now those mice are history

That's the end of my story
and here's a lesson for you
It's one thing to have an idea
and another to carry it through

November 22

For, after all, put it as we may to ourselves, we are all of us from birth to death guests at a table which we did not spread. The sun, the earth, love, friends, our very breath are parts of the banquet . . . . Shall we think of the day as a chance to come nearer to our Host, and to find out something of Him who has fed us so long?
— Rebecca Harding Davis

Giving thanks is one course from which we never graduate.
— Valerie Anders

November 23

If we cannot climb to the mountain top
With those whom the world calls great,
If we cannot join in their lofty work
Nor share in their high estate,
We can sing a song as we pass along
Through the toiling crowds below,
And its notes may fall on some listening ear
With a balm that little know.
— Fannie Herron Wingate

November 24

Do not pray for easy lives. Pray to be stronger men. Do not pray for tasks equal to your powers. Pray for powers equal to your tasks. Then the doing of your work shall be no miracle, but you shall be the miracle.
— Phillips Brooks

November 25

The only way to pass any test is to take the test. All tests on every level are always repeated one way or another until you pass.
— Marlo Morgan

Risk! Risk anything! Care no more for the opinion of others, for those voices. Do the hardest thing on earth for you. Act for yourself. Face the truth.
— Katherine Mansfield, *Journals*

November 26

If You Should Hear A Song

If you should hear a song
Out in the meadow loud and clear,
Have no fear, He is there,
Calling His children dear.

He whispers and cradles all the world.
His voice, it is handsome, old and new.
The melody heard is that of love,
And those who listen hear it true.

The day may be stormy;
It seems it is His wrath.
Through all of your pleading it is cold.
But who can read that Mastermind,
And who doubts His heart of gold?

If you should hear a song
Out in the meadow loud and clear,
Have no fear, He is there,
Calling His children dear.

A man who waits to believe in action before acting is anything you like, but he's not a man of action. It is as if a tennis player before returning a ball stopped to think about his views of the physical and mental advantages of tennis. You must act as you breathe.
— Georges Clemenceau

November 28

If you don't have responsibilities, you don't grow strong enough to handle them.
— Bishop Alexander P. Shaw

Thank God every morning when you get up that you have something to do that day which must be done, whether you like it or not. Being forced to work, and forced to do your best, will breed in you temperance and self-control, diligence and strength of will, cheerfulness and content, and a hundred virtues which the idle never know.
— Charles Kingsley

November 29

The infinite joy of touching the Godhead is easily attained by those who are free from the burden of evil and established within themselves. They see the Self in every creature and all creation in the Self. With consciousness unified through meditation, they see everything with an equal eye. I am ever present into those who have realized me in every creature. Seeing all life as my manifestation, they are never separated from me. They worship me in the hearts of all, and all their actions proceed from me. Wherever they may live, they abide in me.

When a person responds to the joys and sorrows of others as they were his own, he has attained the highest state of spiritual union.

— Bhagavad Gita 6.28–32

November 30

God be in my head,
And in my understanding;
God be in my eyes,
and in my looking;
God be in my mouth,
and in my speaking;
God be in my heart,
And in my thinking;
God be at my end,
and at my departing.
— Sarum Missal

December 1

To make some nook of God's creation a little fruitfuller, better, more worthy of God, to make some human hearts a little wiser, manfuller, happier, more blessed, less accursed! It is work for a god.
— Thomas Carlyle

You have not lived a perfect day, even though you have earned your money, unless you have done something for someone who will never be able to repay you.
— Ruth Smeltzer

December 2

We cannot see God until our heart is like an eagle instead of an owl, able to see the sun. Here is the point of life and of morality: to grow eagles' eyes. Our lives are a process of growing the necessary organs for our destiny. That is the reason why God is such a stickler about morality, not because he wants to control our behavior, but because he wants us to become the kind of people who can see him and thus experience infinite joy. Love longs to spend itself, longs to give itself to a perfected beloved. We must learn to be holy to satisfy God's desire, Love's desire, to spend itself on us.

— Peter Kreeft, *Back to Virtue*

December 3

We often visited Ellen's homeland, where our children had no trouble becoming attached to the Danish scene. When I asked our son how he could communicate with the Danish children with whom he played, he said, "We can't talk together, but we can laugh together."
— Victor Weisskopf

December 4

July 14, 1861, Camp Clark, Washington

My very dear Sarah,
My love for you is deathless, it seems to bind me with mighty cables that nothing but Omnipotence could break, and yet my love of Country comes over me like a strong wind and bears me unresistibly on with all those chains to the battle field. I have but few and small claims upon Divine Providence, but something whispers to me — perhaps it is the wafted prayer of my dear little Edgar, that I shall return to my loved ones unharmed. If I do not my dear Sarah, never forget how much I love you, and when my last breath escapes me on the battle field, it will whisper your name.
But, O Sarah! If the dead can come back to this earth and flit unseen around those they have loved, I shall always be near you; in the gladdest days and in the darkest nights . . . always, always, and if there be a soft breeze upon your cheek, it shall be my breath, as the cool air fans your throbbing temple, it shall be my spirit passing by. Sarah do not mourn me dead; think I am gone and wait for thee, for we shall meet again.

The writer of this letter, Major Sullivan Ballou of the 2nd Rhode Island, was killed in the Civil War at the first Battle of Bull Run.

December 5

Weather-beaten by age, sometimes we are like the earth's crust, hardened with dried apathy, all the feelings completely petrified. But somehow far, far below the layers and strata, the very marrow of ourselves is alive, still warm and soft, ready to erupt at any moment. So we are yet an active volcano waiting for the time to erupt.

Sometimes, yes, very often, we feel empty like a cave eroded by wind and rain, where only loneliness echoes and reaches its rhythmic resonance. We shrug our shoulders, cock our heads, raise our eyebrows, sometimes nodding and sometimes shaking our heads, but all in vain. But we know that God is the only visitor there to see us when we are desperately in need of someone. Then in the hollow vacuum of our hearts where even dreams are absent, He will pour the beautiful message of life, inviting us to drink a nectar of love and elixir of truth.

— Won Pak Choi

December 6

If there is a sin against life, it consists perhaps not so much in despairing of life as in hoping for another, and in eluding the implacable grandeur of this life.
— Albert Camus

Not for the mighty world, O Lord, tonight,
nations and kingdoms in their fearful might —
Let me be glad the kettle gently sings,
Let me be glad for little things.
— Edna Jaques

December 7

If I could say just one thing before I die, it would be this: We die at every moment. Let us not wait for death to wake us up. Let's not stare at life with vacant eyes: let's wake up. Let's realize that most of what we hold so dear will not last, that the precious gift of life that we have in this precious moment will not come back. Let us live now. Let us change now. Let us love now.
— Haydée Watt

December 8

No matter how big or soft or warm your bed is, you still have to get out of it.
— Grace Slick

This is the art of courage: to see things as they are and still believe that the victory lies not with those who avoid the bad, but those who taste, in living awareness, every drop of the good.
— Victoria Lincoln

December 9

Being married and having children has impressed on my mind certain lessons, and most of what I am forced to learn about myself is not pleasant. The quantity of sheer impenetrable selfishness in the human breast (in my breast) is a never-failing source of wonderment. I do not want to be disturbed, challenged, troubled. Huge regions of myself belong only to me. Seeing myself through the unblinking eyes of an intelligent, honest spouse is humiliating. Trying to act fairly to children, each of whom is temperamentally different from myself and from each other, is baffling. My family bonds hold me back from many opportunities. And yet these bonds are, I know, my liberation. They force me to be a different sort of human being in a way I want and need.
— Michael Novak, *The Family Out of Favor*

December 10

Anyone who is strongly connected to God can become a life-giving object, even though that life is not visible to the human eye. You may not become a sun, but you can at least become a lighthouse in the dark.

You do build in darkness if you have faith. When the light returns you have made of yourself a fortress which is impregnable to certain kinds of trouble; you may even find yourself needed and sought by others as a beacon in their dark.
— Olga Rosmanith

December 11

As it is, we are bolting our lives, gulping down undigested experiences as fast as we can stuff them in because our awareness of our own existence is so superficial and so narrow that nothing seems to us more boring than simply being.
— Alan Watts

December 12

We need to work on the central core of the human being rather than only on problems of the environment, outer space, or material and scientific advance. What we need is an increase in the average level of awareness, an awareness which comes from an examined life in the Socratic sense. Curle thinks that most people seem to have a greater belonging-identity than real awareness. The identity of their self is rooted in what belongs to them, whether these belongings are material things, education, or people; and what they belong to, a family, profession, religion, society, etc. But the core of a person lies in the total sense of self behind the often distracting activities of mind and emotion. To the extent that we are self-aware, we are liberated from obsessive self-concern; we are more able to turn to other people and to situations outside our immediate concerns. Thus the concept of awareness includes as an inseparable element the sense of social involvement, an empathy with suffering, and a capacity to relate warmly to other people.
— Ursula King, *The Spirit of One Earth*

December 13

I find the great thing in this world is not so much where we stand, as in what direction we are moving: To reach the port of heaven, we must sail sometimes with the wind and sometimes against it — but we must sail, and not drift, nor lie at anchor.
— Oliver Wendell Holmes

The best way to avoid a bad action is by doing a good one, for there is no difficulty in the world like that of trying to do nothing.
— John Clare, *Fragments*

December 14

Sing songs that none have sung
Think thoughts that ne'er in brain have rung
Walk in paths that none have trod
Weep tears as none have shed for God
Give peace to all whom none other gave
Claim him your own who's everywhere disclaimed
Love all with love that none have felt and brave
The battle of life with strength unchained.
— Yogananda

How Great Thou Art

O Lord my God, when I in awesome wonder
Consider all the works Thy hands have made,
I see the stars, I hear the rolling thunder,
Thy pow'r thro'out the universe displayed.

Chorus: Then sings my soul, my Savior God to Thee:
How great Thou art, how great Thou art!
Then sings my soul, my Savior God, to Thee;
How great Thou art, how great Thou art!

When thro' the woods and forest glades I wander
And hear the birds sing sweetly in the trees,
When I look down from lofty mountain grandeur,
And hear the brook and feel the gentle breeze.

Chorus: Then sings my soul, my Savior God to Thee:
How great Thou art, how great Thou art!
Then sings my soul, my Savior God, to Thee;
How great Thou art, how great Thou art!

December 16

Notwithstanding the poverty of my outside experience, I have always had a significance for myself, and every chance to stumble along my straight and narrow little path, and to worship at the feet of my Deity, and what more can a human soul ask for?
— Alice Jones

December 17

The eye of love makes every person in the world friendly and attractive.
— Sai Baba

Love thy neighbor, even when he plays the trombone.
— Jewish saying

December 18

It may be we shall touch the Happy Isles,
And see the great Achilles, whom we knew.
Tho' much is taken, much abides; and tho'
We are not now that strength which in old days
Moved earth and heaven, that which we are, we are, —
One equal temper of heroic hearts,
Made weak by time and fate, but strong in will
To strive, to seek, to find, and not to yield.
— Alfred, Lord Tennyson

Bring me my bow of burning gold!
Bring me my arrows of desire!
Bring me my spear! O clouds unfold!
Bring me my chariot of fire!
I will not cease from Mental Fight,
Nor shall my Sword sleep in my hand,
Till we have built Jerusalem,
In England's green and pleasant Land.
— William Blake, *Milton*

I see America, not in the setting sun of a black night of despair ahead of us, I see America in the crimson light of a rising sun fresh from the burning, creative hand of God. I see great days ahead, great days possible to men and women of will and vision.
— Carl Sandburg

December 20

My parents always told me that people will never know how long it takes you to do something. They will only know how well it is done.
— Nancy Hanks

December 21

We are the music makers,
We are the dreamers of dreams,
Wandering by lone sea-breakers,
And sitting by desolate streams; —
World-losers and world-forsakers,
On whom the pale moon gleams;
We are the movers and shakers,
Of the world forever, it seems.
—Arthur O'Shaughnessy, *Ode*

I speak to the black experience, but I am always talking about the human condition — about what we can endure, dream, fail at, and still survive.
— Maya Angelou

December 22

The most important function of education at any level is to develop the personality of the individual and the significance of his life to himself and to others. This is the basic architecture of a life; the rest is ornamentation and decoration of the structure.
— Grayson Kirk

Chia Jên / The Family (The Clan)
A healthy family, a healthy country,
a healthy world — all grow outward
from a single superior person.
— I Ching

December 23

But where was I to start? The world is so vast, I shall start with the country I know best, my own. But my country is so very large. I had better start with my town. But my town, too, is large. I had better start with my street. No, my home. No, my family. Never mind, I shall start with myself.
— Elie Wiesel

December 24

A life of reaction is a life of slavery, intellectually and spiritually. One must fight for a life of action, not reaction.
— Rita Mae Brown

Don't wait for your "ship to come in," and feel angry and cheated when it doesn't. Get going with something small.
— Irene Kassorla

December 25

As the dew-drop dangling on the top of a blade of grass lasts but a short time, so even the life of men; Gautama, be careful all the while!

A life so fleet, and existence so precarious wipe off the sins you ever committed; Gautama, be careful all the while!

A rare chance, in the long course of time, is human birth for a living being; hard are the consequences of actions; Gautama, be careful all the while!

— Uttaradhyayana Sutra 10.1–4

December 26

An education isn't how much you have committed to memory, or even how much you know. It's being able to differentiate between what you know and what you don't. It's knowing where to go to find out what you need to know; and it's knowing how to use the information you get.
— William Feather

Who dares to teach must never cease to learn.
— John Cotton Dana

December 27

Over the years I have developed a picture of what the human being living humanely is like. He is a person who understands, values, and develops his body, finding it beautiful and useful; a person who is real and honest to and about himself and others; a person who is willing to take risks, to be creative, to manifest competence, to change when the situation calls for it, and to find ways to accommodate to what is new and different, keeping that part of the old that is still useful and discarding what is not. When you add all this up, you have a physically healthy, mentally alert, feeling, loving, playful, authentic, creative, productive human being; one who can stand on his own two feet, who can love deeply and fight fairly and effectively, who can be on equally good terms with both his tenderness and his toughness, know the difference between them, and therefore struggle effectively to achieve his goals. The family is the "factory" where this kind of person is made. You, the adults, are the people-makers.
— Virginia Satir, *Peoplemaking*

DECEMBER 28

He that has light within his own cleer breast
May sit i'th center, and enjoy bright day,
But he that hides a dark soul, and foul thoughts
Benighted walks under the mid-day Sun;
Himself is his own dungeon.
— John Milton

Do not lay up for yourselves treasures on earth, where moth and rust consume and where thieves break in and steal, but lay up for yourselves treasure in heaven, where neither moth nor rust consumes and where thieves do not break in and steal. For where you treasure is, there will your heart be also.
— Matthew 6.19–21

The story of love is not important — what is important is that one is capable of love. It is perhaps the only glimpse we are permitted of eternity.
— Helen Hayes

I Never Saw a Moor
Emily Dickinson

I never saw a moor,
I never saw the sea;
Yet know I how the heather looks,
And what a wave must be.

I never spoke to God
Nor visited in heaven;
Yet certain am I of the spot
As if the chart were given.

December 31

It's not what we say any more, it's not even so much what we do any more. It's completely and entirely who we are. And that is why we must look deeply into ourselves. Each and every one of us has to ask ourselves, either I am an empty vessel through which God's love can come in, or else I am trying to get something done. Because the truth of the matter is, when we really ask to be empty vessels through which God can operate, plenty will get done. More will get done than you can possibly imagine. It will not, however, be done by us. It will be done through us.
— Marianne Williamson

ACKNOWLEDGEMENTS

Bennett, William J., ed. *The Book of Virtues*. New York: Simon & Schuster, 1993.

Bennett, William J., *Our Children & Our Country*. New York: Simon & Schuster, 1988.

Covey, Stephen R., *Daily Reflections for Highly Effective People*. New York: Fireside, 1994

E. Paul Hovey, *The Treasury of Inspirational Anecdotes, Quotations and Illustrations*. Westwood, New Jersey: Fleming Revell Company, 1959.

Gross, John, ed., *The Oxford Book of Aphorisms*. Oxford: Oxford University Press, 1983.

Kidder, Rushworth M., ed. *Shared Values for a Troubled World*. San Francisco: Jossey-Bass Inc., 1994.

L'Amour, Angelique, ed., *A Trail of Memories*. New York: Bantam, 1988

Maggio, Rosalie, complied. *The Beacon Book of Quotations by Women*. Boston: Beacon Press, 1992.

McWilliams, John-Roger and Peter, *Life 101*. Los Angeles: Prelude, 1990.

Morgan, Carol, *Heirlooms*. New York: Macmillan, 1967.

Platt, Suzy, ed. *Respectfully Yours*. Washington, D.C.: Library of Congress, 1989.

Safir, Leonard and Safire, William, *Leadership*. New York: Simon and Schuster, 1990.

Simpson, James, compiled. *Contemporary Quotations*. Binghamton, N.Y.: 1964

Warner, Carolyn. *The Last Word*. Englewood Cliffs, NJ: Prentice Hall, 1992.

About the Editor

Debby Gullery grew up in Montreal, Canada, and currently resides in Westchester County with her husband and three children. She has a background in marriage counselling and has conducted workshops and seminars on marriage preparation and enrichment. She currently serves as the New York metropolitan area chairwoman for the Women's Federation for World Peace, a non-profit organization dedicated to strengthening the family as the foundation for peace building.